PATIOS, BALCONIES & WINDOW BOXES

HAZEL EVANS

OCTOPUS BOOKS

Contents

Illustrations by
Lindsay Blow: 28, 29, 41, 48-49, 53, 57, 60, 61, 64, 65, 68, 69, 73, 84, 88-89, 93
Chris Forsey: 5, 8, 9, 13, 16, 17, 20, 25, 33, 36-37, 45, 77, 80-81

Acknowledgements
The following pictures were taken especially for Octopus Books:
Michael Boys 6-7, 42, 43, 62, 82, 83, 86-7; Jerry Harpur 10, 50-1 63, 66-7, 71 below, 79; Neil Holmes 11, 14-15, 18-19, 26; George Wright 54, 59, 71 above, 90-1.
The publishers also acknowledge the help of: Octopus Library 27, Harry Smith Horticultural Photographic Collection 75, 94; Jessica Strang 23, 55.

First published in Great Britain in 1984 by
Octopus Books Limited
a division of the Octopus Publishing Group
Michelin House, 81 Fulham Road,
London SW3 6RB

This edition published in 1989

Produced by Mandarin Offset
Printed and Bound in Hong Kong

INTRODUCTION

Gardening in a confined space — on patios, on balconies or in window boxes and containers — can be one of the most rewarding ways of growing things. And it is far less likely to become the chore, or the worry, that running a full-scale garden can be. It is flexible; you can move your containers from one spot to another to catch the sun, group them for instant effect or, by singling one out, turn a plant into a showpiece. You can choose your soil to suit whatever kind of plants you want to grow. There are no problems about having acid-loving plants like azaleas and heathers, for instance, in an area that is unsuitable for them, all you need to do is to provide them with exactly what they want in their own container.

Patios and balconies tend to create their own mini-climate which is more sheltered than in a conventional garden, so you can take chances with things that are not fully hardy in this country, wrapping them up against the elements if there is a sudden cold snap. There's the challenge too of gardening against the odds, defying the rules of nature to produce your own fruit and vegetables with the help of growing bags and containers, even using them as part of the overall decorative scheme. The reward for your labours tends to be more immediate, for plants that are cossetted in this way tend to produce more quickly.

Mini-gardening of this kind gives you a marvellous chance to brighten up ordinary urban items like walls, window ledges and entrance porches. And we've all looked up at a bleak block of flats and seen what a difference just one balcony ablaze with plants in bloom can do. Container gardening will bring your favourite plants nearer to your living area, no need to walk down the garden in wet weather to take a look at them, they're there, right by your window instead. All they ask in return is regular loving care; once properly planted, dead-heading and feeding and watering are all you have to remember for, like household pets, your container-bound plants rely on you to provide them with food and drink.

Few people realize the potential growing space they have around them, even in the most cramped town conditions. Still fewer ever find out just how much fun there is to be had growing things in this way. Small scale gardening is much more under control than the conventional plot. Weeding is reduced to a minimum, digging becomes a thing of the past. Indoor plants can spill over to the outside, linking your home and your mini-garden, making living out of doors a sheer delight. So don't look upon gardening in a small space as a limitation. Instead see it as a delightful challenge.

BASICS OF SMALL SCALE GARDENING

LINKING THE GARDEN WITH THE INTERIOR

It's amazing how you can give the impression of extra space in a house or apartment with a patio or a balcony outside if you make a practice of linking the two together with visual tricks. The first and most obvious one is colour. Simply painting the end wall of a balcony white to match the white paintwork round a window tends to lead the eye out of the room to the distance beyond. But it can be more subtle than that. Take one shade of blue, for instance, and use it in a more positive form around the door or window, and in a mistier version (by simply adding in white) to the patio or balcony wall. This will not only link the two but make the distance between them seem longer than it actually is.

Pattern can be used in the same way: there are many

wallpapers on the market that have a trellised effect, and if this is matched by the real thing on the side walls outside, this too will link the two areas successfully. Another even more sophisticated way of using pattern is to duplicate the flowers on a wallpaper with the living versions outside. Colour too can be used with the aid of plants; the pink of a curtain fabric can be picked up with geraniums, petunias and other bedding plants, or, even more striking, a contrast colour can be chosen to create a dazzling effect.

Sometimes an item of furniture in the room can be duplicated in the patio or balcony outside. This is particularly easy if you choose cane furniture which is light and simple to move in and out. Blend the inside with what goes on outside by growing trailers and climbers round a doorway, so that it is not so pronounced. In summer, morning glories can be grown in pots on both sides of the doorway. A similar idea can be worked with window boxes. You can have matching boxes on each sill, echoing one another. Another way to link the interior of a house with the garden area beyond is with a particular plant. A palm-like plant like the dragon tree grown indoors can be complemented by a *Yucca gloriosa* outside to give a Mediterranean look.

8 PLANNING HOW TO USE SPACE

The first question you need to ask yourself when deciding what to do with the small space at your disposal is what exactly is it going to be used for? Is it simply a view from a window or a decorative addition to a window sill or doorway of your home? Or are you able to use it as a sit-out place in summer, a place to potter around or entertain friends? These considerations need to be taken into account when planning your beds, pots and containers, especially fixed boxes, and where they are to be placed. Aspect matters too. A patio or balcony that gets the full sun all day — an unlikely proposition in town — needs a different kind of planting to one in which you have to cope with shade. Shade also varies from time to time during the year as the sun alters its path across the sky, and what may be heavily shaded during the winter months may have enough sun to cope with bedding plants in summer. An area that gets early morning sunshine may well be used at breakfast time more than in the evening, while one on which the sun goes down will be a natural spot for barbecues and parties and needs landscaping accordingly. Prevailing winds, and especially wind tunnels caused by neighbouring high-rise buildings, may cause problems and need screening off.

Planning ahead before you buy will save you money, especially cash spent on expensive plants that might not be happy in the place in which you put them, a heavily shaded

Plan for a north-facing patio area.

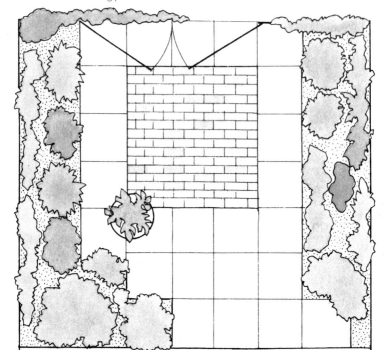

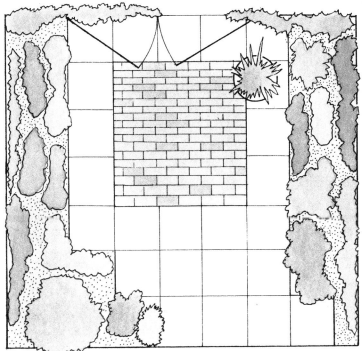

Plan for a south-facing patio area (the ideal direction).

spot for instance. The easiest way to get things right, first time, is to draw up a plan of your plot, however small, on graph paper, using the largest scale you can manage. Knowing that each square represents say 20cm (8in) will save you a great deal of time measuring and calculating. Having drawn up the basic outline of the plot, you can cut out shapes to represent fully grown trees and shrubs in coloured paper, and move them around on the plan until you group them to your satisfaction and can draw them in (see illustrated plans on these pages). If you are allowing for a sitting out area, it pays to cut out shapes for garden or dining furniture too.

Then comes the planting. A north-facing patio like the one shown on the left needs a different planting plan to the similar south-facing one above. In the north-facing patio, *Hydrangea petiolaris* and *Jasminum nudiflorum* are planted against one wall with hedera and philadelphus on the other, all of them plants that can stand some shade. The shrubby plants and the bedding plants are grouped on the side borders where they will catch all the sun available. The container is as far from the shade of the house as possible so it too can get maximum sun. The south-facing patio, on the other hand, features wisteria and a vine as climbers, and makes use of the sunshine with a fan-trained fruit tree against the west wall. It is this western wall that gets the full impact of the sun and so plants that thrive in full sun should be used there.

WALLS AND SCREENS Flowers can easily be grown on a wall by setting up containers on it and filling them with plants. Use wire hanging baskets suspended from brackets or special half baskets which screw into the wall. A line of these can be used effectively to link a container on a patio to a window box on the first floor. Window boxes or plant troughs carried on brackets fixed to the wall will give larger masses of flowers and retain water more effectively.

Plants which climb by twisting, like clematis, or with tendrils, like sweet peas, need support. Fix horizontal wires up the wall to vine eyes driven or screwed into place, or use plastic clematis net or a lightweight diamond-shaped trellis. Fix these supports to vertical 2cm (1in) battens fastened to the wall and the climbers can twist themselves around the support without any help. Heavier squared trellis should be used for free-standing trellis work, such as a screen, which should be nailed or screwed to posts driven into the ground and attached to existing walls to make it steady.

A low divider wall can be planted by putting window boxes or troughs on the top and trailing plants down from them. A

divider wall can be built from reconstructed stone, which is
made from powdered stone and cement. The pieces are made
so they slot together and no bricklaying skill is needed to use
them. Build a stone wall with two faces and a gap between
which can then be filled with earth and planted up.

Pierced concrete screen wall blocks, in a variety of designs,
are ideal for the sides of patios since they give shelter yet still let
in the light and air. They come with special pilaster blocks for
making pillars at either end of the wall, and a wall up to 2m
(6ft) high and 3m (10ft) long can be built in a garden without
reinforcement. Start with a level foundation. Measure the
length, allowing 9mm (³⁄₈in) for the mortar thickness between
each block, and start with the pillars at both ends. When you
have got three or four pilaster blocks in place, start laying the
screen blocks from both ends to the middle. It is important to
check horizontal and vertical lines constantly while you are
working, taking special care that pillars are vertical. These are
then finished off with special capping blocks. There are coping
blocks available too for topping off your screen which can then
be planted with climbers.

PATIO SURFACES

Patios can be constructed from anything from a layer of hardcore, rolled flat, to the most expensive York stone. Hardcore is difficult to maintain. Almost as cheap is concrete (one part cement, two parts sand, four parts aggregate), which can have colour added to the mix to make it a warm red, brown or yellow. Lay the concrete on a 15cm (6in) layer of compressed hardcore, and mark it off into squares with the edge of a board about an hour after the concrete is laid, just as it is beginning to set. You can increase the effect by dribbling a different coloured concrete into the grooves when the patio has set. Pre-cast concrete slabs are available in different thicknesses, sizes, colours, and shapes — including circular and hexagonal. More expensive but more effective are the reconstructed stone slabs, in which the makers have used real stone to reproduce the shape of the stone surface. These should have a base of hardcore, followed by a layer of builders' sand, or a weak, dry cement mix — nine parts of builders' sand to one of cement or lime. Check that each slab is level as it is laid, and fill in the small gaps between the slabs with brushed sand or the weak cement mix.

You can get a chequerboard effect by using two different colours or shades of slab, or, as illustrated below right, by leaving out some of the slabs and planting up the gaps with herbs which give off a sweet scent as they are walked over, such as the low-growing lemon scented thyme (*Thymus citriodorus*) or the mat-forming chamomile (*Anthemis nobilis*).

Bricks make a warm, mellow patio surface which goes well with a brick-built house. You can use second-hand house bricks, flat or on their sides, or pavoirs, the half-thickness paving bricks used by the Tudors for their garden paths. They can be laid in conjunction with stone slabs (top right), or on their own in a pattern (centre right). Put down a 5cm (2in) layer of sand, then a polythene sheet to act as a damp-proof membrane. Leave some drainage holes round the edges of the patio. Finish off by brushing fine sand into the joints.

Cobblestones also give a period flavour to a patio. You can buy the stones from a builders' merchant. Start with a concrete base, at least 7cm (3in) thick. When this is hard, start laying the cobblestones. Mix a little mortar, three parts builders' sand to one part cement. Place it on the concrete and set the stones in it, pressing them level with a wooden float so that more than half of each stone is embedded. Do not mix more mortar than you can use in an hour. When you have finished an area, leave for three to four hours, then clean up the stones with water and a stiff brush.

You may yearn for grass on your patio but the best alternative may be a creeping plant that makes a good grass substitute. This will be essential for the patio surface under a deciduous tree that bears berries. It will save sweeping up the fallen berries and prevent the patio surface from staining.

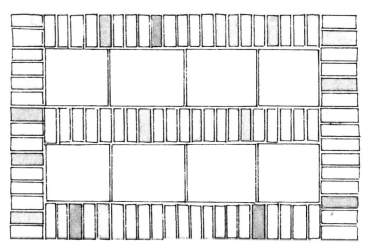

Bricks and stone slabs.
Brickwork in a circular design.

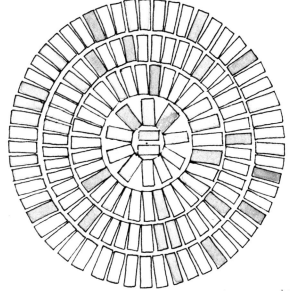

Stone slabs with low-growing plants.

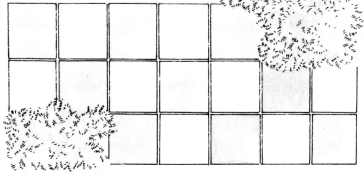

14 PERMANENT PATIO BEDS

Beds that are made permanently round the patio enable you to have plants at different levels, giving variety. They are also useful for the elderly and the disabled. A bed 60cm (2ft) high and about the same depth back to front is ideal for wheelchair users and one about 90cm (3ft) high can be used for the elderly or disabled who can walk.

Large patio beds contain a great weight of soil which must be kept in place by properly constructed walls. A brick-built bed looks attractive but needs to be professionally made if it is of any height, preferably with 23cm (9in) walls. All permanent beds need a firm foundation and, if the ground is soft, a hardcore or concrete base should be put down first. The construction of raised beds from concrete blocks or stones is not, however, difficult for the amateur. Unless you intend to build over 10cm (4in) high, piers are not needed for beds made from concrete blocks, but you must give strength to the retaining walls by building them in some form of bond, such as stretcher, where the vertical joints of each course come over the middle of the blocks in the course below. You can get decorative concrete blocks with an imitation stone face on one side in a number of thicknesses, and a standard 46 × 23cm (18 × 9in) in width and height. These fit in with the dimensions of

bricks, so you can mix some bricks into the walls if you wish to marry the beds in with a patio that has been built of brick.

You will find that extra dimensions can be added to the patio by the use of permanent beds, each of different size and height, the deepest beds being used for plants which need a good depth of soil. For shallow-rooting plants you can make up boxes from small aggregate-faced walling units, which come in various lengths, and from 30-60cm (1-2ft) high. The ends are ready-mitred to give neat corners. Make up each box by bedding it on to the patio surface with a little mortar, and joining the corners with more mortar. Before filling permanent patio beds with soil, line them with polythene sheeting so that the water in the soil does not mark or break down the bricks or blocks.

Making a raised bed with a chunky stone front is easy for the amateur. Fit the stones together as best you can, then fill in the gaps with mortar. Any defects in construction only add to the rustic charm. Later you can put some soil and small plants into some of the holes in the front. Don't forget that you can fill your raised bed with lime-hating plants, such as rhododendrons and heathers, enjoying them even in an area where the garden soil is too chalky for them by using peaty soil or by giving the bed walls of peat blocks.

16 CONTAINERS FOR PLANTS

Containers for the patio come in a great variety of shapes — boxes, tubs, bowls, urns and barrels — all made in different sizes and materials. Plastic is the cheapest and the most popular. It is lightweight, does not break easily, and keeps the soil moist. As well as the usual troughs, urns, boxes and pots, it is moulded into plastic spiral planters to take small alpines and herbs, and in stackable tower pots suitable for strawberries. Sunlight, however, turns it brittle.

Glass fibre is moulded and coloured to imitate old-fashioned lead and stone troughs and urns. They are light, keep the compost moist, and are strong, long-lasting, and repairable. Reconstituted stone, which is powdered stone mixed with concrete, is used to make good imitations of the traditional urns, bowls and vases. They look good anywhere, but are heavy even before they are filled with compost, and should be used with care on balconies.

Concrete is used for making large cone- and dish-shaped planters which go best with modern architecture. Both concrete and reconstituted stone containers should be weathered before being used for lime-hating plants. Terra cotta, made from clay, is a sympathetic material, but it cracks or breaks easily. It is often used for strawberry barrels, and for

Versailles tub   Strawberry pot

small 'parsley pots' with holes in the side which can be planted with herbs (below centre).

Wood is a material which goes with any surroundings, and it keeps the roots of the plants warm. But unless hardwood, such as elm, teak, or oak is used, it must be treated to prevent it rotting. It can be varnished, painted, or treated with a wood preservative which is not toxic to plants. It comes in the form of half-barrels, tubs, boxes, troughs, and the Versailles tub (below left), which often has sliding wooden panels so that from time to time you can open a side of the tub, remove the old compost, and replace it. In this way, at Versailles, they kept plants such as orange trees growing for decades.

The newest material for containers is resin-bonded cellulose fibre. It is cheap and lightweight, and its peaty appearance and colour gives it a natural look. Its life span is uncertain, although the makers give a two-year guarantee against 'moisture deterioration'. You don't have to stick to purpose-made containers. An old wooden wheelbarrow, with holes in the bottom and painted in a bright colour, makes an amusing container. Old wine or beer barrels with holes drilled in them look good (below right). And the old-fashioned stone sinks come complete with a drainage hole, their thick clay walls retaining the heat, and they are suitable for miniature gardens or rockeries. If you like to change the design on your patio and need to move your containers about with ease, fit castors on them, or place them on a manoeuvrable platform (below). It is advisable to position a wooden tub clear of the ground by putting it on a few bricks. This allows air to pass freely underneath and prevents the timber from rotting.

Wooden barrel on castors

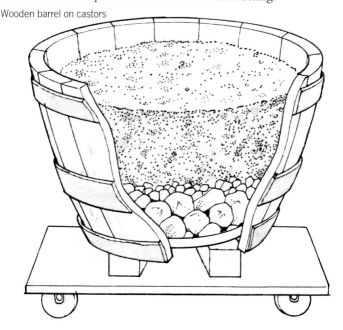

18 WINDOW BOXES

Ideally a window box should match up with the length and depth of your window sill and not get in the way of the window itself. But if the box is too shallow, the plants will suffer from not having enough soil and will need watering more frequently. Aim at a minimum soil depth and width of 15cm (6in) which means that the inside of the box should be 18cm (7in) deep to allow a space at the top for watering.

There's a wide choice of boxes to be found now in the shops. There are, for instance, convincing imitation lead boxes, made from glass fibre, which is light, strong and rot-proof but expensive. At the other end of the price scale are thin plastic boxes which are also lightweight and rot-proof but they do not last forever as constant sunlight makes the plastic brittle and they crack. Extra long plastic boxes can distort and be difficult to handle when they are filled with soil, so they are better used with lighter soil-less composts. Both fibreglass and plastic boxes retain moisture better than wooden ones and some come with their own drip trays and automatic watering. Wooden window boxes go with every type of house style and seem to complement the plants better than any other material but those made from softwood will rot quickly. Avoid them if you can and go for hardwood — elm, oak, ash or teak which should last for many years without needing any preservative paint or varnish.

If you cannot find a box to fit your sill or balcony, it is a relatively simple matter to make your own boxes. Wood is the ideal material — hardwood of course. Cut two pieces the requisite length and two box ends and join them with brass screws. For the bottom of the box use pieces of 5 × 2cm (2 × 1in) battens, screwed to the endpieces but with a small gap between each to allow for drainage. It is a good idea to put 'legs' on each corner of the box to allow the water to drain away; sawn off pieces of cotton reel are ideal for this.

Apart from wooden and plastic boxes, it is possible to find some attractive versions in terra cotta and reconstituted stone. But these should only be used in a permanent site, and are rarely suitable for window sills. They also have a tendency to be cracked by frost.

Whatever kind of box you use, make sure that it is fastened securely and is level if it is on a ledge. Window boxes are best backed up by brackets or chains. Balcony boxes can usually be supported by iron brackets and there are some attractive wrought iron versions to be found. Remember watering problems when you site window boxes overlooking a street; it is all too easy to drench passers-by. If for some reason a box is not suitable, try a row of flower pots fronted by a plank of wood fixed on the edge instead. Or you can place flower pots in a window box on a bed of pebbles and moist peat so that you can ring the changes more often. You can also achieve a framing effect by hanging baskets on either side of the window.

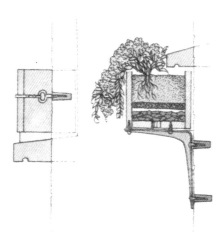

Above the sill, use wall plugs and galvanized wire to keep the box level (left), and brackets with rustproof screws in wall plugs beneath the sill (right).

GROWING BAGS

These are plastic bags which vary from about 90 × 30cm (3 × 1ft) downwards in size and contain a peat-based compost with added nutrients. You place the bag on your balcony or patio, cut holes or slits on the upper surface, plant up and water. They can be used for any shallow-rooting plants — tomatoes, peppers, aubergines, cucumbers and marrows, strawberries, French beans, lettuce, herbs or flowers. Do not use them, however, for deep-rooted crops such as carrots or beetroot.

Once you have planted the bags up, it is vital to maintain the watering. Most people under-water growing bags, but if you are afraid of making the plants waterlogged, choose a version that has its own water reservoir, or poke a few drainage holes in the sides. Or you can buy special plastic trays for watering growing bags, and a form of drip equipment, especially useful for when you go on holiday.

Use your growing bags to their full capacity to get the best value from them. You can under-plant tomatoes with lettuce, for instance, if you wait until the tomatoes are established and growing well first. The nutrients you start off with in a growing bag are not always enough to last a full season, and at some stage you might have to add other fertilizers. When you start feeding and how much fertilizer to give are critical to successful cropping. Instructions on this are usually printed on the side of the growing bag. Follow them exactly and do not be tempted to over-feed or you will get too much vegetation and not enough vegetables.

Some growing bags have unsightly printing or advertising on them. There are various ways of obscuring this: you can paint the entire bag one colour using any exterior emulsion paint, or you can edge the bag neatly with a double row of bricks and cover the top with pebbles or peat to hide the plastic altogether.

Tall plants such as tomatoes or cucumbers will need to be propped up in some way in the growing bag. If it is not possible to string them up to something, special rigid supports can now be bought that are made especially for containers of this kind. Don't throw your growing bag away at the end of the season, it can be re-used provided you do not plant the same crop. But remember that all the nutrients will have been used up and you will have to put some new fertilizer in before you start again.

Growing bag production is now a highly competitive business and you will often find the bags sold at very cheap prices. Check on these, for they can be cheaper to buy than bags of soil-less compost, so it may pay you to get some purely to use the contents for potting up your plants. Small versions of the growing bag are available which are useful for growing houseplants indoors. They are particularly good for indoor herb gardens; plant parsley, chives, thyme and sage in a small bag and you have a mini herb garden. Give mint a bag of its own as it will only take over the other plants.

MAKING THE MOST OF CONTAINERS A few

containers filled with flowers can turn a patio or a balcony into a garden in no time at all, and even a single tub of carefully chosen plants can give a country air to a dreary town scene. Troughs of plants can be put all along the outside edge of a balcony or, if there is room, round all three sides to give the effect of a series of flower beds. If your balcony is too small for this kind of arrangement, consider hanging window boxes from the top of the railings and filling them with trailing flowers. If your balcony has a parapet wall, put window boxes or plant troughs along the top. In either case, however, make sure that they are properly secured so that they cannot come adrift or topple.

A container has a great many advantages over a conventional flower bed. It allows you to grow tender, exotic plants, bringing them in when frost threatens, and to plant lime-haters, such as rhododendrons, in a chalky area. The doorway to a town house can be softened by a well-placed container of flowers. Suspend hanging baskets from brackets either side of your front door, or from the roof of a porch to give a welcoming splash of colour. Set a neatly clipped bay tree or a pair of conifers in tubs on either side of the front step for a more formal look. Even the side of a flight of steps can be softened by the use of small containers — rectangular shapes or squared-off tins are ideal for this since they fit smoothly against the wall. Old food or oil cans are often ideal for this purpose and provided they are painted in bright colours, their original use will never be noticed.

Always buy the largest containers that you have the space for; the larger the container the easier it is to maintain since it will not need watering so often. But bear weight in mind when you are dealing with a balcony, for the extra height that you get with the width of a large tub means that it takes up a great deal of soil, and therefore a great deal of weight. It is a good idea to choose containers that can be mounted on castors if you plan to grow some prize-winning plants. You can then shift them around as the sun moves, or take them in out of the frost. Troughs with castors can also be used to grow moveable hedges, planted up with conifers or other bushy items such as *Lonicera nitida*.

If you are going to look down on your containers, attractive colour arrangements can be made with bedding plants. Don't forget the attraction too of one or two colour schemes — a garden in containers that is all silver and white looks very attractive. Always cluster small containers together for maximum effect, don't string them out or they will have very little impact. If they are to be painted, then small containers look best painted in one colour scheme.

Try the container in various positions when empty to get the best effect. If you are putting it on a paved area, place it across a join so that the water can seep away.

A large decorative glazed tub provides an interesting container.

SOILS AND COMPOSTS In an ordinary garden, the roots of plants are free to go in search of nutrients that they need. But plants confined in small beds or in containers can use only the nourishment that you give them in the compost you use, so care must be taken to see that plants get the food they want. A small container planted up with garden soil, for instance, would probably not give the plants enough food, so unless you are prepared to give a liquid food right from the start, it is better to begin with a special compost.

Soil-less composts are now popular because they are light, sterile and clean to handle. They are based on peat and contain a complex mix of nutrients and trace elements. Different grades are available for different purposes such as seed sowing or potting out. Or you can now get a multi-purpose compost which is an average grade and can be used for anything. But soil-less composts do have some disadvantages. Because they are so light they do not give the same root anchorage as soil-based composts, and a pot with a top-heavy plant in it is easily blown or knocked over, especially if the compost has become dry. Getting the moisture right can also be a problem. Some composts soak up water like blotting paper and the plant roots almost drown, others dry out readily and are difficult to get wet again once this has happened.

Soil-less composts are ideal where weight is a problem, on a balcony or roof garden for instance. Otherwise the alternative is John Innes Compost, a soil-based mix. You can buy bags of John Innes from any garden supplier, it is not a brand name. John Innes No. 1 is suitable for small plants and seedlings, John Innes No. 2, containing twice as much fertilizer, is general-purpose for most pot plants, and No. 3, with treble the fertilizer in it, should be used for vigorous greedy feeders like tomatoes and sweet peas. You can also get John Innes seed compost, and special mixes to cope with lime-hating plants like summer-flowering heaths and heathers, rhododendrons and azaleas.

If you want to do so you can make your own John Innes formula compost this way: mix seven parts by bulk of soil with three parts of peat. Then mix in two parts by bulk of sharp sand. To every bushel (36 litres or 8 gallons) of this mixture add 110g (4oz) John Innes Base Fertilizer plus 28g (1oz) chalk if you are making the No. 1 mix. Double the amount of chemicals for No. 2 and treble them for No. 3. If you are making up a compost for lime-hating plants, double the amount of peat, and omit any chalk, then check your compost's pH with a soil meter. Plunge the metal probe into the compost. The dial reading will show whether the soil is acid or alkaline. Included with the meter is a list of the best pH levels for different plants. Remember if you are using compost in this way in containers, it will be necessary, after a while, to feed your plants. Constant watering, especially with a hose, tends to leach out the nutrients.

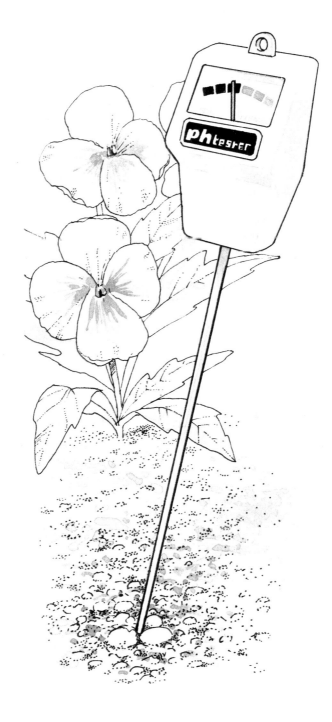

A soil pH meter measures the acidity or alkalinity of the soil.

WHAT TO LOOK FOR WHEN BUYING PLANTS

The first thing to check when you are buying plants is that you are getting what you want. Some garden centres and nurseries tend to be careless about their labelling, and some plants are known by a number of different names, so go by the Latin one which is the most exact and accurate. If in doubt, ask, or check one of the standard reference works; most garden centres have these on sale.

Check the plant before you buy to see that it is healthy. Commonsense will usually tell you this. Any brown or diseased parts are a bad sign, so is a plant that has apparently been trimmed or shorn of a number of branches or leaves. A plant that is growing well has plenty of small buds starting into growth with a lighter-coloured tip to the shoots. Look out for a sturdy plant, avoid a thin straggly one even if it is taller (a temptation with climbers), as it is probably weak and may have been forced too quickly. Short, thick plants are almost always a better buy. Look at the surface of the compost in the pot. Avoid a plant that has some shed leaves on top of the soil, this is usually a sign that it has been allowed to get too dry at some time and has lost its leaves in a desperate attempt to stay alive. A film of green algae over the surface of the compost, on the other hand, means that it has probably been over-watered. Moss or weeds growing in the pot around the plant are also a

Young fuchsia and cyclamen plants.

A healthy chrysanthemum plant in a pot.

sign of poor husbandry by the nurseryman or garden centre and probably mean the plant is old.

Tip the plant out of the pot and examine the roots if you can. You should be aiming at a plant which is ready to move on to a bigger pot, so the root system should just fill the pot that it is in. If the roots are a compacted mass of fibres which have taken on the shape of the pot, then the plant is root-bound, has been kept in a small pot much too long and will take a long time to recover from this treatment. If, on the other hand, you can see no roots at all in the soil, this could be worse. It probably means that the plant has not been grown in the container at all but has been dug up from open ground at the nursery and put into a pot to make it look as though it has been container-grown. Or it could be the plant has been raised from seed in a peat block or pot which has then been put into the container just before sale. There is nothing wrong with this method of raising plants, but you should not buy such a specimen until it has grown into the compost in the container and you are sure that it has survived the transplant.

If you buy a plant early in the season, make sure it is not a straggler left from the year before. Roots hanging from the drainage holes or, worse still, growing through into the ground beneath are an indication of this, as are top shoots which have been trimmed back. Buy young plants rather than old, they transplant better.

RAISING PLANTS FROM SEEDS

Raising from seed is the cheapest way of getting new plants. But it is only worthwhile doing if you need a lot of plants, or you want a variety which you cannot buy as a ready-grown plant. It takes time, patience, and some skill, and if you want only a few plants, and can buy them ready-raised, it is best to do so.

Ensure the seed is fresh; seed packets now carry the date of packing and when they should be used by. Soil-less composts give better germination than the John Innes soil-based composts. For large numbers of plants use plastic seed trays or polystyrene slabs with holes for the compost. For individual plants, use small plastic or peat pots (below), or Jiffy 7s, compressed peat 'pots' which expand on wetting. Soil-less compost should be pressed down lightly with the fingers. Sow the seed as thinly as possible. Do not shake direct from the packet or the seed will be much too thick, and the seedlings will suffer from overcrowding and become weak. For most seeds, use a pair of tweezers, or your finger and thumb, to place them exactly on the compost. Sprinkle a little compost over the seeds, but do not cover too thickly — about 3mm (1/8in) is thick enough cover for most seeds, while some very small, dust-like seeds need no covering at all. When the seed is sown, water the containers by lowering them into a bowl of water for

Peat pots allow direct planting of seedlings without disturbing the roots.

about half a minute, making sure the water does not come over the top. Drain the containers, then cover them. Seed trays can be covered by a sheet of glass and some newspaper. Plastic pots can be covered by an open plastic food bag, held in place with an elastic band under the rim of the pot. During germination you can use a plastic propagator, which is a plastic cover with adjustable vents in the top to regulate the humidity. If using sheets of glass, wipe them clear of condensation every few days. Seeds germinate more quickly with heat. You can get propagators with heating elements in the bottom or you can use the airing cupboard to give them gentle heat. Do not let the temperature rise above 21°C (70°F). Check the containers daily, and as soon as the tiny plants appear, get them into the light, or they will grow straggly and weak.

Transplant the seedlings as soon as they are big enough to handle — they recover quickest when they are tiny. Pick the seedlings up by the leaves, never handle by the stem, which is very delicate at this stage. Disturb the roots as little as possible. Water very gently with a fine rose, then leave the seedlings in a shady spot to recover from the move. Finally put them out in the sun.

GUIDELINES FOR PLANTING

Before planting up a container, check that there are enough drainage holes in the bottom because a waterlogged plant will drown. Some makers expect you to drill or cut your own holes, and with many plastic containers the holes have not been cut properly. All the drain holes should be covered to prevent compost being washed out. Small pieces of broken clay pots are ideal for this. Place a piece concave side down over each hole and put a layer of small stones round it to keep it in position. Add a little peat, then half fill the container with moist compost.

When planting bulbs in containers, crock the pot in the usual way, half fill with moist compost, then put in a layer of sharp sand for extra drainage. Press the bulb firmly onto this base, then fill the pot with compost, firm lightly with the fingers, and level off the compost 19mm (¾in) below the rim of

Bulbs should rest snugly in the soil (left); not as on the right.

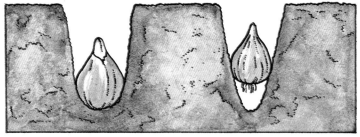

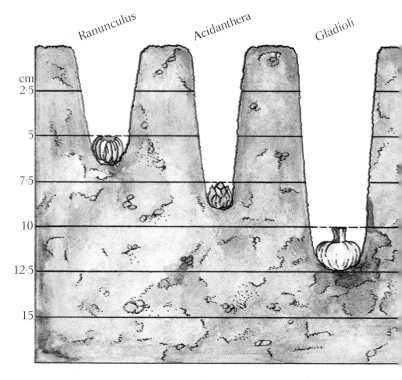

Ranunculus   Acidanthera   Gladioli

cm
2·5

5

7·5

10

12·5

15

the pot. Water, cover the pot with a piece of glass or slate to stop mice eating the bulb, and put the pot in a cool place till a shoot appears, when it must be brought into the light. Crocus corms need a period of cold before they will germinate, and can be left outside in the autumn. Bulbs which are to be planted in a flower bed should be put in compost to the correct depth (see illustration below).

If you are moving a plant to a larger pot, check that it is ready for potting on by examining its roots. Hold the plant in place with a couple of fingers on top of the compost, turn it upside down, and gently tap the rim of the pot on the table or work surface (page 65). The plant and root ball should then slide gently from the pot. If you can see roots circling the compost and filling most of the pot or hanging from the bottom, the plant is ready for potting on. If you see no roots, slide the plant back and leave it for a few days.

Before potting on, remove any crocks caught up in the roots at the bottom of the root ball, and gently tease out roots around the outside. Place the plant in its new container and check for height. The surface of the compost should be about 19mm (¾in) below the rim of the new container. Gently press the plant in place, and fill in the gap round the plant with fresh compost. Water, and put the plant in the shade somewhere for a day or so to settle in its new home.

When planting up a plastic tower pot with strawberries, separate the units, plant them up, and fit the tower back

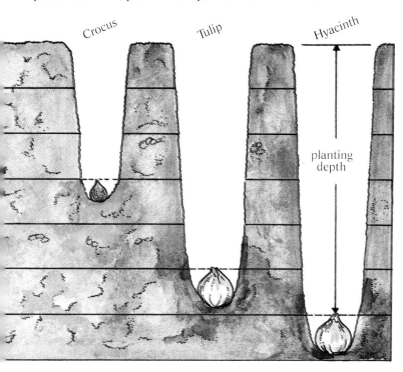

Crocus   Tulip   Hyacinth

planting depth

together again after watering. The strawberry plants go into the little half cups. Drainage crocks are not usually needed, as the plastic mesh at the bottom of each unit is fine enough to keep most compost in place. A terra cotta strawberry barrel, however, needs crocking in the usual way. Put compost in the barrel to the level of the first holes, insert plants through the holes from the outside, cover with compost, firm with fingers, and carry on up the barrel until all the holes are full. Finish off by planting more strawberries in the open top and watering well. Plastic spiral planters, useful for herbs or alpines, should be checked for drainage holes before planting. You can make these with a hand drill if they are not provided. Crock each hole, and plant from the bottom of the spiral to the top, filling in with compost as you go. If you plant one of these spirals with strawberries, the runners hang down and can be rooted into the compost further down the spiral. Strawberry barrels do not have to be restricted to strawberries — you can plant them with alpines or succulents as well, or a combination of all three. Plant wall-hung troughs as for pots.

If the plant needs a stake, this should be put in position at the time of planting, so the roots are not damaged. For soft-stemmed plants, such as geranuims, use a cane and tie with raffia. For hard-stemmed plants, such as trees and shrubs, use thin timber stakes, treated with a preservative non-toxic to plants, and tie with a special plastic tree tie (4) which allows a gap between the stake and the tree. The stake should be planted with the tree (1-2) and be perpendicular to the ground. Firm the soil all round the base after planting (3).

Do not pot small plants straight into a large container, or the plant will sit in the middle of a mass of cold damp compost which will eventually turn sour. Plants must be potted on in stages; when their roots are just beginning to run out of compost is the time to move them on. Do not leave it too late, or the roots will form a tangled mass and the plant will run out of food and become pot-bound. As you move each plant, move the label with it, or you will find yourself with a mixed heap of labels and plants you cannot identify. If you are planting grafted stock (fruit trees, roses, shrubs) make sure that the point of grafting is 2cm (1in) or so above the surface of the compost, or you will have suckers growing from the rootstock. Identify the graft point by a slight swelling in the stem and a change of direction. If you are making a mixed planting in a window box, a trough or a large container, get all your little pots together and put them on the compost surface to make sure you like the arrangement. When you are ready, start with the largest plants, which are usually in the centre. Before removing each plant from its pot, check that the hole you have made is big enough by inserting the plant in its pot in the compost. Do not cram the container with plants, or there will be too much competition for the available water and food, and the weakest plants will suffer and die.

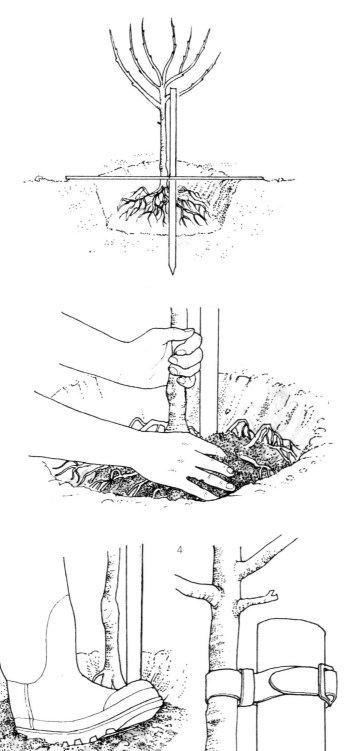

HOW TO PLANT A HANGING BASKET

Hanging baskets crammed with flowers are the most effective form of container gardening, but they are also the most public, and unless you get the planting right, the results of your mistakes are on display. Make sure that whatever you hang your basket from is able to hold the weight of the basket plus its plants and wet soil, and that you will be able to water the basket on average once a day, and if possible give it a good soaking in a bucket of water once a week. You can get plastic hanging baskets, some with built-in drip trays, which are easier to plant than the traditional wire basket, since they do not need lining, but they do not look as good as the real baskets. These consist of an open framework made of galvanized or plastic-covered wire, and they come in different sizes and shapes. Try to find a deep, bowl-shaped basket, rather than the saucer-shaped one, which does not hold so much compost and dries out too quickly. Work on the basket while it is being held steady jammed into the top of a bucket or tub. Traditionally, the basket is then filled with sphagnum moss, which holds the compost in place, allows for drainage, and gives the basket a natural look. Unfortunately, fresh sphagnum moss is often hard to find, and even if you are able to obtain a supply, it is difficult to line the basket with the moss without leaving

gaps through which the
compost can fall. You can use
polythene sheeting instead,
but this is unattractive to look
at. Use a cellulose fibre bowl
liner. Poke a few drainage
holes in the bottom with a
sharp knife, then drop it into
the basket. Fill it to within
5cm (2in) of the rim with
John Innes No. 3 compost.
Do not use soil-less compost,
which dries out too quickly.
Plant your basket in early
summer with flowers just
coming into bloom. Make a
hole in the centre of the
compost and insert one or
two tall plants. Make holes
round the edge for trailing
plants, and insert each at an
angle so it falls over the edge.
Add another 2cm (1in) of
compost, and some small
plants in the gaps. You can
insert some small trailing
plants into the sides of the
basket through holes cut in
the liner. Finally soak the
whole basket in a large bowl
of water for about half an
hour, and your basket is ready
for hanging out. Keep a close
eye on the basket for signs of
drying out. You will have to
water at least every other day,
and in a hot dry summer you
may have to increase the rate
to twice a day. Give liquid
fertilizer once a fortnight, and
once a week soak the whole
basket in a bucket of water.
The baskets on these pages
contain some of the favourite
plants: fuchsia, begonia,
lobelia, calceolarias,
morning glory, stocks, cup-
and-saucer plants, asters,
busy lizzie, geraniums,
chrysanthemum, cornflowers,
saxifraga and alyssum.

WATERING AND FEEDING A plant in the garden can send its roots in search of water and nourishment, but a plant in a container is entirely dependent on what it is given. A container full of roots has very little room for anything else, so its reserves are small and even these can disappear through the porous walls of a container. Proper watering and feeding is vital to the life of container growing plants, and most people under-water and under-feed. How much water to give depends on the weather, the season, and the plant. On a hot, windy day a plant with a lot of vegetation is using water rapidly, and will need watering daily. Do not wait until the plant is showing stress by wilting. In the summer, water in the early morning or late evening, and keep water off the leaves; drops of water act as a lens and the sunlight will scorch.

Plants need nitrogen, phosphorus and potassium for good growth. Other minerals, such as sulphur, calcium and magnesium, are also necessary in smaller quantities. Even smaller amounts of other minerals, known as trace elements, must be present in the soil; these include iron, boron, zinc, copper and molybdenum. These minerals are all naturally present in the soil, but the plants gradually absorb them so feeding is essential.

Check the compost regularly. A finger tip lightly dragged over the surface should show some dampness. Water until surplus runs from the bottom of the container, then stop. Too much water will flush nutrients out of the compost. Sprinklers save time but they should be used sparingly as they waste water. Capillary matting allows you to leave plants unattended for days. Put the pots on the matting and lead it to a water reservoir next to it. You can also insert capillary wicks into the bottom of pots through the drain holes. Strips of capillary

matting can be led from a bucket of water to plant containers at a lower level. Push the strip into the top 1cm (½in) of compost. Self-watering planters have their own reservoir of water. All these devices let you leave plants unattended when you go away on holiday. But if you are growing lime-hating plants, such as rhododendrons, azaleas and heathers, in a hardwater area, you must not use tap water, as the calcium builds up in the compost in the container. Use rainwater, or softened or distilled water.

Water before feeding your plants with fertilizers so that the chemicals are spread evenly through the compost. Always use a balanced fertilizer containing nitrogen, potassium and phosphorus, unless you are giving a specialized feed. Powder or granular fertilizers are spread on the surface of the compost and taken in whenever you water. Liquid fertilizers are diluted and watered in. Foliar feeds are the most difficult to apply, and are normally used for remedying a chemical deficiency, such as iron- or lime-hating plants. They are sprayed on the leaves. Fertilizer sticks, or pellets, are labour-saving though expensive. They are pushed into the top of the compost and left there. They gradually release the chemicals into the compost.

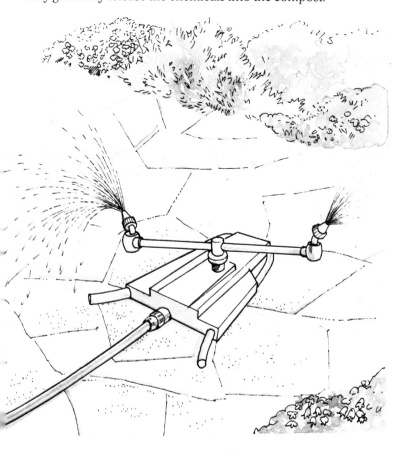

CONTROLLING PESTS

Pest	Symptoms	Treatment
Adelgids	– Sap-suckers on conifers	Malathion
Aphids	– Green and black fly	Malathion
Birds	– Eat fruit buds and fruit	Netting
Box sucker	– Malformed leaves on Box	Malathion
Chrysanthemum leaf miners	– Tunnel into leaves	Gamma-HCH
Codling moth	– Maggots in fruit	pbi Fenitrothion
Earwigs	– Eat flowers and leaves	Gamma-HCH
Froghoppers	– Froth (Cuckoo spit)	Malathion
Holly leaf miner	– Tunnels into Holly leaves	Gamma-HCH
Leafhoppers	– Mottled leaves	Malathion
Lilac leaf miners	– Tunnel into syringa leaves	Gamma-HCH
Lily beetle	– Eats leaves and flowers	Malathion
Mealy bugs	– Waxy wool on plants	Diazinon
Poplarbeetles	– Eat poplar leaves	Gamma-HCH
Red spider mite	– Mottled leaves, spiders	Systemic insecticide
Rhododendron bug	– Mottled brown leaves	Gamma-HCH
Rhododendron leafhopper	– Lesions in buds	Gamma-HCH
Scale insects	– Sooty patches on leaves	Malathion
Slugs	– Eat plants – slime trails	Methiocarb
Stem and bulb eelworm	– Plants soften and rot	Garden hygiene
Thrips	– Silver mottling of leaves	Malathion
Weevils	– Eat roots of pot plants	Gamma-HCH
Whiteflies	– Look like tiny moths	Pyrethrum
Woodlice	– Grey, hard-coated, eat plants	Gamma-HCH
Woolly aphids	– White woolly tufts on twigs	Systemic insecticide

DISEASES

Anthracnose of willow: Small black cankers on shoots and brown spots on leaves, which become distorted. Treatment: Spray with a copper fungicide.

Azalea gall: Leaves are replaced by fleshy galls which later turn white. Treatment: Remove and burn galls as they appear, spray with zineb.

Black spot: Brown and black spots on rose leaves, which then turn yellow and drop off. Control by fortnightly spraying throughout the summer, varying the fungicide.

Blindness: Bulbs grown in containers which fail to flower. Buds may appear, then rot. Cause is not enough water, or, less often, too much water. Control by keeping compost just damp.

Bud drop: Flowers, especially sweet peas and wisterias, losing their buds. Caused by dry compost.

Clematis wilt: Clematis plants, especially the large-flowered varieties, wilt and die. They usually grow again from the base next spring. Spray with copper.

Downy mildew: White tufts on the leaves of vines, and shrubs. Spray with zineb.

Peach leaf curl: Unsightly red blisters on leaves of peaches and ornamental prunus trees. Spray with Bordeaux Mixture just before bud burst and leaf fall.

Powdery mildew: A fungal disease attacking a variety of plants, showing itself as a white powder on leaves and shoots. Control by sulphur dust or dinocap spray.

Rhododendron bud blast: The flower buds on rhododendrons turn grey or black. The disease is transmitted by the rhododendron leafhopper, and control is by eliminating these pests (see Pests Chart).

Rust: Red-brown patches on leaves of roses. Difficult to control, usually better to remove and destroy the affected plant before it infects others.

Silver leaf: A fungal disease affecting plums, rhododendrons, and other shrubs. The leaves turn silvery and sometimes brown. Cut out and destroy infected branches, paint fungicide on the cuts, and give a fungicide spray.

FURNISHING A PATIO OR BALCONY

patio, unless it is covered by a roof, must take account of the weather and the fact that a bright sunny day can turn within minutes into a rain-drenched disaster. So your patio furniture has to be either easily portable or totally weatherproof. Stack-away furniture such as deck chairs, collapsing card tables, folding chaise-longues are fine provided you have somewhere to store them when they are not in use. Keep fold-up items well oiled at the joints as even a short shower of rain on them may make them rust. Cane furniture is cumbersome, though attractive, and is only really suitable if you are able to use it indoors as well. Otherwise it is safest to make sure that everything can be left out, even when it rains. Victorian chairs and tables in cast iron look good on any sort of patio, but need time spent in keeping them painted so that the rain cannot reach the metal underneath. Modern reproductions, which are made of cast aluminium, look the same but will not rust. The chairs tend to be uncomfortable, but this can be remedied with a few small cushions, which can easily be covered with attractive waterproofed fabric. Cast aluminium chairs, like cast iron ones, are surprisingly heavy. There are lighter versions in similar patterns to be found in the shops in white plastic. They are much cheaper but they are not so attractive in complicated shapes and usually look better in plain designs. Wooden benches with matching tables go well on a patio in country surroundings, especially when they have been left out to weather a little. Go for teak if you can, which is a wood that carries its own oil as a form of waterproofing, or elm which distorts slightly as it weathers to produce some interesting shapes. But before you buy, check the fastenings. It is not uncommon to find a very expensive teak bench that has been put together with steel screws which will rust. Try to find one where wooden pegs and wedges are used for the fastening, or brass screws. Swing seats are very comfortable and give a touch of luxury to a patio, but, even if the cushions are covered in plastic, the springs and fastenings will rust in the rain so it is necessary to have a waterproof cover for it, preferably one which is easy to fit. Portable barbecues are no trouble to carry in and out, but if you are going to do a lot of entertaining on the patio, consider making a built-in barbecue at one end. You can build it in brick or in reconstituted stone, with a simple metal grid for cooking the food. You can make one of the piers about 1m (3ft) wide, and finish it off with a piece of slate or marble which can then be used as a work surface for preparing food. You can even build a cupboard below to store the fuel.

The backdrop to your patio furniture is another consideration. You may want a Mediterranean look with white-painted brickwork and cane or cast-iron furniture; or a Japanese look with bamboo fencing and stone benches. Remember to plan lighting too; paraffin flares on poles are ideal.

THE CHOICE, USE AND CARE OF PLANTS

FLOWERING TREES AND SHRUBS
Trees and shrubs that give colour in the form of flowers are doubly welcome in a small space, and fortunately there are literally hundreds to choose from. The ideal situation to aim at is a plot or a series of plantings where something is in flower in every season of the year. And if you can ensure that most of them are evergreen, so much the better. Azaleas have attractive, glossy dark green leaves and some spectacular flowers. And if you are gardening in a small space it is usually possible, even around a patio, to make a special bed of acid compost that suits them. Camellias are good value too, and provided you give them a relatively sheltered spot, they will do well, often coming into flower as early as February.

Buddleia davidii 'Dartmoor'

Rhododendron 'Britannia'

Small fruit trees give the double bonus of flowers in the spring then a crop later on, and the Morello cherry is ideal for a north wall, since they will thrive in these conditions. Fan-trained, they make an attractive focal point anywhere. The golden yellow flowers of forsythia are a welcome sight in late winter and, coralled in a container (it should be at least 60cm [2ft] wide), it can be kept under control and shaped into an attractive bush. Don't forget the hardy fuchsia (*F. magellanica*) which has pretty, though smaller flowers than the indoor variety and can be clipped into a mini-hedge.

If you want to attract wildlife, then the smaller Buddleias such as *B. globosa* 'Lochinch' is compact in its habits, has grey foliage and beautifully scented lavender flowers. Hydrangeas can look attractive, but if you want to avoid the more common hortensia, try the lacecap varieties instead, *H. macrophylla* 'Blue Wave' for instance. Lilac, viburnum and the mock orange, philadelphus, will all fit into a small space. The senecios, especially *S. maritima*, give attractive silvery colouring with vivid yellow, daisy-like flowers in summer. They're invaluable for container and window box plantings but they can be killed off by a really hard frost if you are unlucky, so protect them if frosts seem likely.

Finally, the prunus family gives a welcome sign of spring, and the flowering cherry is probably the best known. However, *P. subhirtella* 'Autumnalis' is an even better choice for it produces its frilled bell-shaped flowers in the autumn, and sporadically through the winter too. And if you have space for a small specimen tree that you can show off, then a weeping pear *Pyrus salicifolia* 'Pendula' could make a really attractive focal point.

Greenery all year round, topped up with some seasonal colour, is the general aim in any kind of small-space gardening. Since you are working with a tiny area everything has to earn its keep. First plan your background furnishings, the items that will stay put all year through and give a backdrop or, in some cases, a foreground of greenery. A surprisingly large selection of evergreen trees can be found in dwarf or even in miniature window box versions. Conifers are an example. And hardworking perennial climbers such as ivy can make a useful contribution, being easily used as trailing plants to front window boxes or balconies.

If you are dealing with an area such as a balcony or a patio rather than simply planting a container, it is a good idea to indulge in some basic colour perspective to help make the available space seem larger than it actually is. Use dark blue-greens of evergreens such as *Chamaecyparis lawsoniana* 'Minima Glauca' or *Jupinerus communis* 'Compressa' Blue Star round the edges, where they will appear to recede, with golden or lighter green plants such as *Hedera helix* 'Buttercup' in the foreground.

Remember that permanent plants are, as their name suggests, going to be *in situ* for a long time so give them a flying start with the very best mix of soil you can find. Small trees and other heavyweights need a good loamy soil rather than something lightweight to anchor them.

Take shape into account when choosing your permanent plants. If you are going for a country look, then sprawling or rounded trees and shrubs are fine, but in a formal garden a specimen fastigiate or columnar tree, or one that is pyramidal can look very effective, especially in town conditions. If you are putting permanent plantings into window boxes, do take into account the height they will reach or you may find yourself peering out over the top of what is essentially a small hedge.

Permanent plants for window boxes include aubrietia, low-growing hardy evergreens; lily-of-the-valley, plants which like partial shade and will need thinning from time to time; short bushy lavender (*Lavandula compacta* 'Nana'), which grows only 15cm (6in) high and is useful for the edges of boxes. Creeping Jenny (*Lysimachia nummularia*) is a ground-cover plant with bright yellow flowers which will look good in a box of primary colours; miniature roses also come in many colours; and *Vinca minor*, the lesser periwinkle, is useful for both window boxes and hanging baskets as it quickly fills an area and bears bright blue flowers. *Senecio compactus* has silver-grey foliage, but it will need clipping.

Seasonal planting starts with bulbs which are either taken out when they have finished flowering and stored, or left in place if there is the space for them. They give special pleasure in early spring when there is a dearth of colour around. Then comes the turn of the herbaceous perennials if you have a large enough space to accommodate them, and finally the traditional bedding plants which can often be bought cheaply in local street markets to top up whatever is already in place. It is a good idea to switch colour themes from one year to another for a change of scene. If you have enough room to store them during the winter months when they must be protected from frost, then half-hardy items such as fuchsias and geraniums give a great deal of colour for their money. Remember that indoor plants can be given a new lease of life in mid-summer. Put them out of doors for a rest.

Dwarf conifers and ivies provide year-round greenery in window boxes.

Walls are all-important when you are gardening in a restricted space for they give you a valuable added dimension on which to grow things. And that's where climbers and wall shrubs come into their own. Don't forget that they can be used for screening purposes too.

One of the most sturdy and useful of all climbers is *Hydrangea petiolaris*, for although it is not an evergreen, its glossy green leaves are slow to drop at the end of the year and early to return the next. Its delicate and lace-like caps of white flowers are unlike those of the hydrangea that you see in florist's shops and, best of all, it will thrive on a north-facing wall. Clematis are valuable flowering climbers to have, especially on a balcony or in a tub. But for the first year or so their delicate, rather brittle stems need watching, for it is too easy at the end of the season to break them accidentally when tidying up a pot or a plot. For sheer bravado in terms of show, try Nelly Moser with boldly striped large petals, or The President, which has large, deep mauve-blue flowers. A clematis mixes well with a climbing rose, using it as a support

Hydrangea petiolaris

and the rose will mark the spot and remind you where you have planted the clematis.

Don't forget the attractive morning glory (*Ipomoea*), an annual climber with convolvulus-like flowers that are usually seen in blue but can be found in pinks, purples and reds too. And the passion flower (*Passiflora*) is surprisingly easy to grow despite its exotic looks, and generally hardy too. For scent you can't beat one or other of the many honeysuckles (*Lonicera*) and jasmine, another easy climber to grow.

Remember for the best results with climbers don't plant them too near a wall or fence, or you will restrict their roots. The same goes for wall plants. And one of the most rewarding of these is ceanothus, an evergreen shrub with pretty fluffy blue flowers. Another useful shrub that benefits from being planted by a wall is *Cytisus battandieri* which has scented golden-yellow flowers. *Kerria japonica* 'Flore Pleno', if it is kept in bounds, will reward you with double yellow flowers just when you need them in late spring and, for the rest of the year, its bright green stems look attractive, especially against a white painted wall.

CONIFERS AND EVERGREENS

These are the essential furnishings that turn a one-season garden or window box into an all year round proposition. They are the trees and shrubs, however small, that will stay put. Fortunately even the smallest window box or sink garden can have a small evergreen to go with it. But apart from choosing miniature or dwarf trees, there is another alternative with patios and balconies in mind, for you can always pick a specimen that is naturally slow growing. Keeping it in a container will restrict its rate of growth still further. Conifers are best for this and are normally very good tempered provided that you water them regularly when they are first planted. But one situation they will not tolerate and that is industrial pollution.

Two members of the large juniper family are ideal for planting in window boxes or tubs. *Juniperus communis* 'Compressa' is extremely small and only reaches 30cm (12in) high after ten years so it is an ideal candidate for a window box, while *Juniperus chinensis* 'Pyramidalis' has a similar columnar appearance and blue green foliage, but it will reach 182cm (6ft) after ten years so makes a good tub or patio specimen. An even narrower conifer is *Juniperus virginiana* 'Skyrocket' which will grow a little taller, but not much. Another good-tempered conifer to use in these circumstances in *Picea glauca*.

In the formal surroundings of a town patio or balcony, those great standbys yew, box and the shrubby form of honeysuckle, *Lonicera nitida*, look splendid when they are clipped into an architectural shape, or trained into something more fanciful. Lonicera incidentally comes in an attractive yellow form called Baggesons gold. Topiary can be done in two ways; by clipping

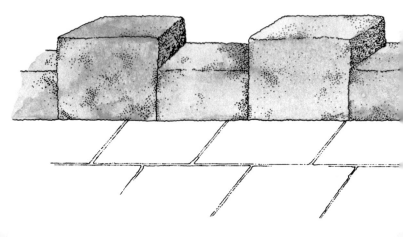

an already grown specimen into a tailored shape or by the judicious use of wire (unravelled coathangers are ideal for this) to turn it into the shapes of birds or animals. Another way that works well inside and outside is to make the shape of an animal in wire and sphagnum moss, then trail a small-leafed evergreen ivy over it.

To give a tropical look to a patio or a balcony you can't do better than choose the *Yucca gloriosa* which will survive the winter well in a relatively sheltered spot — a town patio for instance — or the New Zealand cabbage palm, *Cordyline australis*. Don't forget the hardy evergreen herbs when you are choosing evergreens for a small space, since they will give double value. Lavender and rosemary are two good-tempered evergreens that look very decorative (both can be clipped, topiary fashion if wanted). Just for a change try *Lavandula dentata*, a version of lavender that has toothed leaves. Bay too is already well known both as a specimen and as a form of hedging, and sage also makes a magnificent evergreen shrub. Of course not all evergreens need be green. You will find conifers ranging in colours from blue-green to a rich golden-yellow.

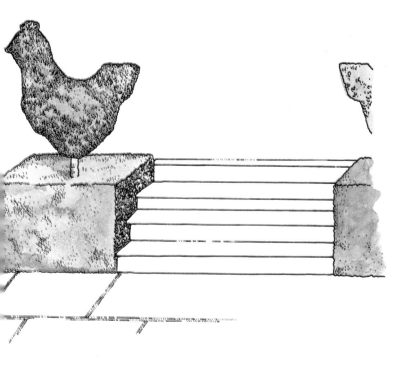

GROUND COVERING SHRUBS Small low-growing
shrubs that can take care of themselves and suppress weeds
make useful ground cover in situations where every centimetre
of space matters and they save a great deal of work at the same
time. If they are evergreen, then they'll give year round
coverage and protection. All the creeping forms of thyme make
attractive and fragrant ground cover, knitting together to form
a tapestry of many colours. There are 20 or more varieties to
choose from but silver posy, Annie Hall, golden lemon thyme
and the silvery grey woolly *Thymus langenosis* are some
reliable types to start off with. Two other herbs, the shrubby
germander (*Teucrium fruticans*) and cotton lavender
(*Santolina chamaecyparissus*), make excellent ground cover
in raised beds and can be used, clipped, as an edging for tubs or
miniature gardens. Chamomile makes a perfect alternative to a
grass lawn and emits a perfume when you tread on it.

In patio plantings some of the heathers are good in this role,
notably *Erica carnea* which is more lime-tolerant and rewards
you with flowers in the winter. And it is worth considering
Genista hispanica, Spanish gorse, which grows low and has
golden yellow flowers. A prostrate version of cotoneaster,
Cotoneaster dammeri, is good for tailored ground covering in
a bed edging a patio, and a version of ceanothus, *Ceanothus
thyrsiflorus repens*, otherwise known as creeping blue

blossom, gives a mound of dense evergreen foliage which is covered in blue flowers in late spring. *Euonymus fortunei*, sometimes called darts blanket, is a good choice of evergreen ground cover if you live near the sea for it can cope with salt-laden winds, and it has attractive reddish-purple flowers. Yet another version of honeysuckle, *Lonicera pileata*, is like *Lonicera nitida* in that it could be mistaken for box, but it grows much lower, with branches that reach out horizontally making a good tailored ground cover. Another useful choice is the Oregon grape, *Mahonia aquifolium*, which is evergreen and has scented yellow flowers in spring and edible blue-black berries in the autumn. If you don't mind a deciduous plant, then choose *Potentilla glabra mandshurica* with its attractive silver-grey foliage and white flowers.

One of the best known of all ground cover plants is *Vinca major*, the periwinkle which grows at great speed and will cover a tub or a window box in no time at all. Another flowering shrub we normally think of in different terms is the hardy fuchsia which, in its dwarf compact version, *Fuchsia* 'Tom Thumb', makes good dense cover, especially in a decorative tub, and has constant flushes of lovely carmine and violet flowers. Small alpine shrubs come to the rescue as well, try *Juniperus procumbens* for instance, which will cover a small area in a fast time.

SHRUBS AND CLIMBERS FOR FOLIAGE AND BERRIES When choosing climbers and shrubs for your plot, don't forget to include at least one or two items that have attractive foliage and/or berries to give much needed colour in the autumn when other things die down. The cotoneaster, for instance, is one of the best-loved wall shrubs because of the vivid fruits it produces. *Cotoneaster* 'Cornubia' has large red berries, while *Cotoneaster franchetii sternianus* produces orange ones or, if you prefer yellow, try *Cotoneaster rothschildianus*. The hawthorn, *Crataegus grignonensis*, sports deep red berries that last for a long time, and there are several trees and shrubs that give you the bonus of two attractions: *Malus evereste*, the French-bred crab apple tree, ideal for growing in tubs, has pretty white flowers in spring, followed by bright red fruits which are edible and which will stay on the bare branches all through winter, and *Daphne mezereum*, a shrub that produces fragrant flowers in early spring and follows these up with attractive red berries.

Another good choice of wall shrub is the evergreen mahonia which has attractive blue-black berries that look good against a white-painted patio wall. Pyracantha, the firethorn, is another shrub that can be relied upon to berry prolifically. A point to watch, incidentally, when using berried trees on a patio or balcony is that it is best to place them in a corner, where the berries when they fall are less likely to be trodden underfoot, staining paving or flagstones.

If you want coloured foliage, the Japanese maples are among the most rewarding of all small trees. *Acer palmatum* 'Senkaki', the coral-barked Japanese maple, is good for a small space, never reaching more than 3.6m (12ft) high. Its bark is, as the name suggests, coral red and its leaves turn an attractive shade of yellow in the autumn. *Acer griseum*, another variety, has deep red leaves in the autumn but tends to grow taller — it can reach 4.5-6m (15-20ft) so it needs more space to itself.

Cornus alba 'Sibirica', Westonbirt red-barked dogwood, is an attractive version of the popular and colourful dogwood that thrives in a small space and, apart from its vivid red stems in winter, has leaves that turn a matching carmine in the autumn. A little known shrub that gives you the double pleasure of colourful berries and colourful leaves is *Callicarpa bodinieri giraldii*. It grows to just over 180cm (6ft) high and is happy in a large tub or planter. It has lilac flowers in early summer and its leaves turn yellow and red in autumn with vivid violet-coloured berries, a happy choice for a patio or balcony garden. The black mulberry, *Morus nigra*, is an attractive proposition: it grows 2.7-3.6m (9-12ft) tall and makes an interesting gnarled shape. Its dark green, heart-shaped leaves are set off by edible orange to purple fruits.

Often it is the cold inhospitable north-facing walls that are neglected in gardens. But in a small area no wall can be ignored. There are a surprising number of shrubs and climbers which enjoy north-facing conditions and provide colour, often when it is most needed, in the winter months. These include *Choisya ternata*, the Mexican orange, which grows to 1.5m (5ft) and produces white scented blossom; *Garrya elliptica*, with long white catkins; and *Jasminum nudiflorum*, a winter flowerer. Foliage can be provided by ivies (*Hedera*) holly (*Ilex*) or vines (*Polygonum*).

Pyracantha atalantoides

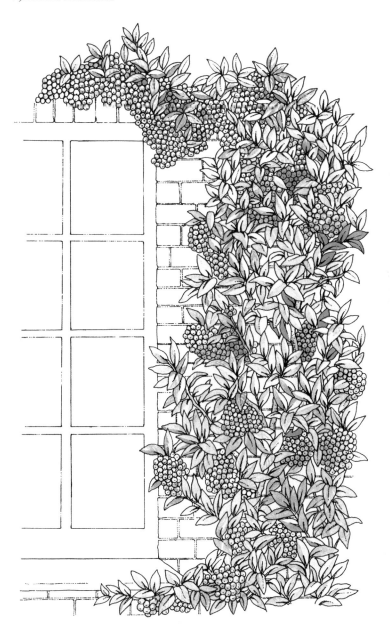

Plantings like trees, shrubs and climbers are likely to be in place for a long time, so it's essential to give them the best possible start in life. Before you begin to plant your climbers, do take the opportunity to fix adequate supports or ties for them while you are able to reach the wall up which they will grow. This saves problems later. Lightweight climbers such as clematis are often best growing up a mesh support of some sort. Or if they are to go in front of a wooden fence, it is a relatively simple matter to fix short lengths of twine or ties to the fence with a household staple gun. Brick walls need proper vine eyes to take ties for climbers. And if you are using trellis in any form, especially if it is free-standing, make sure that it is supported properly or it will act like a sail in the wind.

If you dig in plenty of compost at planting time for your climbers, trees and shrubs, they should be able to look after themselves for some time. The same goes for items planted in tubs or boxes; start them off with a good compost such as John Innes No. 3. Remember to water all newly planted shrubs and trees well at first, especially if they are evergreens. Check them carefully for any sign of pests or disease, especially in early spring when the new growth occurs. As a precaution, spray fruit trees, roses, conifers and ornamental shrubs with a diluted mix of bromophos in oil to kill off unwanted overwintering pests which may be present in the form of eggs or larvae.

Wisteria sinensis

Pruning is necessary for six main reasons: to increase flowers, to alter the shrub's shape, to encourage new growth, to remove dead or weak growth, to lessen leaf area on newly planted shrubs so that the root system can cope with its environment and to alter the flowering season. Prune for shape and to let in light and air to the middle of dense specimens such as yew or box. The time of year when you do this varies according to the variety but basically shrubs that flower in early spring should be cut back after their blooms have dropped. Taking off their lead or header shoots will divert growth to the side buds below and give you a bushy rather than a tall specimen. Dead-heading blooms on all flowering shrubs will help ensure a continuing supply of blooms. Climbers used as trailers or ground cover should be groomed from time to time. Clear away decaying vegetable matter.

Wall climbers will need training to cover the wall or support the way you want them to, and to have their weak shoots cut out to encourage a strong basic framework and to avoid overcrowding. The pruning requirements of the most popular of all climbers, clematis, vary from one type to another. The large-flowered hybrid clematis such as Jackmanii and Comtesse de Bouchard need cutting back hard in November, or in March if they are in an exposed spot, while varieties such as The President and Nelly Moser should be pruned as little as possible since they mainly flower on old wood.

Container grown ivies have been trained on ropes down the front of this house.

PRUNING ROSES Hybrid tea and floribunda roses are pruned to encourage production of new shoots which will give flowers and to produce shaped, healthy plants. Left unpruned, a rose bush will grow tall, producing a lot of thin, straggly, unhealthy shoots and poor, small flowers. They must be pruned every winter, any time from January onwards. It is better to prune too early than too late, since a mild spring can cause the roses to break their buds early, then some young shoots have to be cut off and wasted.

For pruning you need thornproof gloves and a pair of secateurs. Single-bladed secateurs are easy to use, since you can cut with the tip of the blade, and blade sharpening is not critical as you can get a clean cut with a blunt blade. Two-blade secateurs, called parrot bill, cut in the centre of the blade and need careful maintenance. Always cut at an outward-facing bud, with a slope the same direction as the bud, about 6mm (¼in) above the bud (top left). The slope is so that the rain runs off the cut end. Cut too close to the bud and you risk damaging it. Cut too far away and you have a length of wood which can die and rot. Newly planted roses must be cut back drastically to encourage vigorous new growth if this has not been done already by the nursery. Leave two or three shoots, each about 12cm (5in) long.

First stage in pruning is to go over the bush and remove ruthlessly any diseased or damaged wood. Then cut away any dead wood; cut from the end, 2cm (1in) at a time until you come to healthy tissue with a white centre and a thin green rim. Cut out any stems which are rubbing, or crossing the centre of the bush. You are aiming for an open, cup-shaped bush which lets in light and air. When you have done this you will be left with six strong, healthy shoots. Reduce each shoot to about half its length. Any shoots thinner than the rest should be cut back further to encourage thicker growth to about a quarter of their length.

Treat a standard rose, which is really only a bush on a long stem, in the same way, but try to leave the stems the same length, so you get a nice cup shape to the tree. Newly planted climbers should not be pruned, apart from removing any wood which has been damaged in transit. Nor do they need the regular pruning you give to bushes and standards, since you want to encourage high growth. So just remove diseased or dead wood and crossing branches, and cut off any branches which are growing where you don't want them to go. Repeat-flowering climbers generally flower on lateral growths which should be pruned back to a few eyes in the autumn. Young growths should be trained at this time to spiral around the trellis or fence or to grow horizontally. Old flower heads should be removed (unless you want to keep the hips); this will extend the flowering period. Miniature roses need only the removal of dead or diseased wood. Use scissors rather than secateurs.

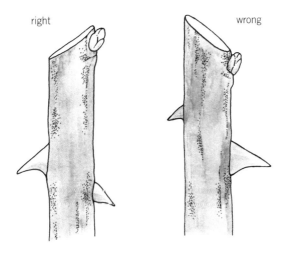

right   wrong

THE CHOICE OF ROSES Roses for the patio or balcony must be chosen with great care. If you pick the wrong variety of rose for your garden, the mistake can be hidden among the rest of the flowers, but a rose on a balcony or climbing the house wall is in the limelight. Try to visit a rose nursery or garden centre from June onwards when the roses are in bloom and can be seen and smelled, rather than buying them in the autumn from a catalogue. Colours in catalogues may not be accurate, and scents vary so much, something listed as 'fragrant' may be too cloying for your taste or so subtle that you cannot detect it at all. This is an important point for patios and balconies as the scent will drift inside in summer with the windows open.

With the exception of miniature roses (which are excellent for window boxes), all roses like deep soil, and if they are to be grown in containers these should be at least 30cm (12in) deep, preferably much more. On a patio, if you can give them access to a deep root run by removing part of the paving where you plant them, so much the better.

There are four types of roses for the small space gardener to choose from (ramblers and shrub roses are not suitable for restricted areas). Hybrid tea roses are the modern bush roses, available in a profusion of colours and varieties which are constantly being added to by the breeders, and they are sold everywhere, in chain stores and supermarkets as well as garden centres. If you are in doubt it is safer to choose varieties such as Peace or Wendy Cussons that have stood the test of time. In theory hybrid tea roses go on flowering right through summer, but some tend to bloom in flushes, with gaps between. Try to find a continuous flowering variety such as Blessings. Remember to dead-head your roses to encourage flowering.

Floribundas are bushes which produce clusters of smaller blooms than hybrid tea roses. They are usually continuous-flowering and the bunches of blooms give good splashes of colour through the summer. They are not generally fragrant, though some new varieties being bred, called floribunda-hybrid tea types, are often sweet-smelling — Margaret Merril, for example. Iceberg, Paddy McGredy and Elizabeth of Glamis are all popular floribundas.

Climbing roses make excellent cover for a wall or a fence and can be used to trail over the side of a balcony. To get the best value for money choose a repeat-flowering variety such as Leverkusen which goes from June through to autumn and will succeed on a north wall. Zephirine Drouhin, Danse du Feu and Ena Harkness are three other well-known climbing roses. Zephirine Drouhin can also be trained as a tall bush or mini-hedge. Miniature roses which grow about 30cm (12in) tall at the most are ideal for flower pots or other containers such as window boxes. There are dozens of varieties to choose from such as Baby Darling which has orange blooms, and the lilac-coloured Lavender Lace. The smallest is the 12cm (5in) Tom Thumb.

Rosa 'Zephirine Drouhin'

GETTING THE MOST FROM YOUR BULBS Given

good basic care, bulbs, corms and tubers are a good investment for the small scale gardener since even a few will provide reliable yearly shows of colour. And with the exception of half-hardy items such as dahlias, begonias and one or two other specimens, your bulbs can stay in place from one year to another without any trouble.

Bulbs are remarkably good tempered and need very little attention apart from good rich soil to begin with. To encourage flowers in the more 'difficult' varieties such as amaryllis, it helps to give them a top dressing of potassium sulphate when the leaves first appear. Bulbs look at their best clustered together rather than strung out, unless they are specimen plants like lilies. And for the purpose of getting the best show, buy a number of one variety rather than one each of several different types.

Bulbs look particularly good when they fill a terra cotta pot on a patio, clustered round the base of a small specimen tree or even planted in a hanging basket which can be used attractively out of its normal season in this way. If you are growing bulbs in containers of any sort, don't forget to continue to feed and water them after they have bloomed. That way you are investing in better flowers for next year for this is the time that the leaves are pumping food back into the bulb to store it. For this reason you should never cut down the foliage

Tying up daffodils after they have bloomed.

after flowering but let it die back naturally. This can be tiresome for the small scale gardener as it makes containers in particular look untidy, window boxes too. If possible copy the professional gardener and bend the foliage down in a simple tidy knot. If this is really out of the question, then lift them very carefully, trying not to break the whiskery roots, and plant them temporarily in a tub (a plastic bucket will do), or heel them in a corner patio bed until they have finally died down.

If every centimetre of space counts, it is sensible to lift your bulbs to replace them with summer flowers and store them somewhere dry and cool. A garage or an attic room is ideal, but with ingenuity you will find other places — the floor of a cupboard without a hot water pipe running through it, for instance, or even under a bed. Put them in trays, making sure that they do not touch each other. First remove dead skins, cut off shrivelled leaves and take off any offsets to dry separately. Tender plants like gladioli and dahlias can be restarted indoors in spring if you have the space, then put out when the danger of frost is past. Other bulbs can easily be forced for indoor use at any stage: plant them in fibre, water them, and keep them in a black plastic bag to exclude light. Once the shoots are 2cm (1in) high, bring them into the light and they should flower a week or so afterwards.

You can increase your stock of bulbs by separating and planting the bulblets that develop around the mother plant.

Tazetta narcissi

COLOURFUL BULBS Carefully chosen, bulbs can be used
to give you effortless colour all year round. They can be set out
in so many ways from the natural look to a formal edging.
Never plant less than five of the same variety, however, or they
will look lost, even in the smallest space. Check on the
eventual height of your bulbs so that you can plan where to
plant them. Daffodils, for example, grow to 45cm (18in).

Starting in spring, crocuses, daffodils and narcissi are the
mainstay of many gardens. If you are using them in a small
space, it pays to look out for the species varieties of daffodils
rather than the full-blown ones. Varieties to use are the
Narcissus asturiensis with tiny trumpets less than 7cm (3in)
long, or the hoop petticoat daffodil *Narcissus bulborcodium*,
which looks good in raised beds and urns. They are also good
for neat edgings to window boxes. Tulips, too, can be found in
all sorts of forms apart from the conventional type. There are
the 'parrot' versions, for instance, which have feathery, often
striped petals and look less stiff.

Glory of the snow, chionodoxa, is an early flowering bulb
that sometimes surprises by coming out when there is still
snow on the ground. Plant it in clusters, and the same goes for
another spring flower, the grape hyacinth, muscari. In early
summer, the unusual *Fritillaria meleagris* has pretty dropping
flowers with coloured freckles on them. It grows very fast and
forms large colonies after a season or so. Bluebells do well and

Crocus and chionodoxa

Lilium speciosum

give a country look to a small patio if you can give them shade.
You will find them listed under scilla in the catalogues and you
can ring the changes and plant pink or white versions (*Scilla
hispanica*) instead of the blue. Lily-of-the-valley, *Convallaria
majalis*, is another shade-loving bulb which quickly forms
colonies.

In midsummer, montbretia and its more florid relative, the
gladioli, which now comes in a dwarf form, take over the scene
and anemones make a colourful addition to a tub or a box.
They can look unexpectedly attractive underplanted round
gladioli which are usually used as specimen plants in a small
area. Lilies make splendid specimen plants in tubs or even in
individual flower pots. They are, surprisingly both hardy and
very easy to grow. The tiger lily, *Lilium tigrinum*, is probably
the best known of the colourful ones, but *Lilium* 'Fire King',
which has a similar colouring, or *Lilium speciosum* 'Grand
Commander', which is a pretty pink, both make wonderful
specimens. If you want creamy-white colouring, look for
Lilium 'Bright Star'. When autumn comes the nerines take
over, with their large pink lily-like flowers, and the autumn
colchicum which is not a crocus but looks like one. Finally the
snowdrops come, *Galanthus nivalis*, appearing in January. If
you want to beat the seasons, however, look for *Galanthus
corcyensis* which blooms in November.

MAINTAINING HEALTHY PERENNIALS

Perennial plants form a useful backbone to the planting of a balcony or a patio since they do not need to be constantly replaced or raised from seed. But it is all too easy to neglect them, for they do need attention in the spring or in the autumn if they are to look their best. Groom them by cutting away decaying foliage and dead-heading flowers and they will reward you with an immaculate appearance. Check them from time to time for growth; perennials in a raised bed may need dividing from time to time. The easiest way to do this is to place two forks back to back in the centre of the clump and then pull them apart (1), then trim off any dead or diseased looking tissue around the inside of the plant or any tough woody crowns in the two pieces before you replant them (2).

Make sure that your perennial plants get off to a flying start with the right soil. If you are planting them in tubs then John Innes compost Nos. 2 and 3 are good choices. Top up the compost with a fresh supply on top each spring, and remember to feed your plant regularly throughout the summer. Check them over from time to time for aphids, whitefly and other unwelcome visitors and always have a spray can or mister of the right chemical to hand to ward off attacks of this kind.

From time to time your perennials will need repotting. The most convenient time to do this is in the spring or in the

autumn if your containers have mixed plantings or permanent plants plus annuals and bedding flowers. Once the latter have died down or, better still, before they are put in place in the spring, tip your perennial plant, plus the root ball of soil surrounding it, out carefully (3), and inspect the roots (small plants can be tipped out of the containers with the support of two fingers around the stem). If the roots are thickly matted together around the outside of the pot and coming through the drainage hole at the bottom, it is time that it was potted on. Choose a container that will give the plant another 5cm (2in) of root space, no more, and prepare the new pot in the usual way, covering the drainage hole with pieces of broken crock. Sprinkle a layer of new compost inside the level that will bring the plant to the correct height in its new home, so that the top surface of the soil comes about 4cm (1½in) below the rim. Centre the plant with its original root ball of soil carefully in the new container then fill up the sides with new potting mixture (4), firm it down and water well. Well-established perennials that do not need to be put into new pots may need some fresh soil from time to time. It's a good idea to scoop out what soil you can from the top in spring, without disturbing the roots, and replace it with some fresh compost to give the plant a fillip. Above all, do remember that container-grown perennials need feeding too.

HARDY FLOWERS FOR LONG-TERM PLANTING

Hardy flowers come in two categories; the perennial ones that go on from year to year without much trouble apart from occasional tidying up and dividing, and the annuals which you can either start from seed or buy from garden centres or nurseries in the spring. Perennial hardy flowers are the basis of a small garden and are usually listed under herbaceous perennials in the nurseryman's list. They include many of the old favourites such as michaelmas daisies, golden rod and other cottage flowers. There are some varieties, the sunflower for instance, which come in both an annual and perennial form, the sweet pea is another. Some of the most popular flowers, the marigold, lavender and ladies' mantle (*Alchemilla mollis*) are also regarded as herbs, and indeed in medieval times many flowers, including violets and pansies, were used in cooking and for decoration on salads rather than purely for garden decoration.

Choose your perennial and annual hardy flowers to give your garden a theme. You could have a cottage-garden look, featuring delphiniums and lupins at the back of the bed or the centre of a container, sweet Williams, marigolds and Canterbury bells around the perimeter. For a daisy theme you could mix the shasta daisy (*Chrysanthemum maximum*) with rudbeckia, which is otherwise known as black-eyed Susan, and use the real daisy, *Bellis perennis* 'Dresden China', with

pink tips to the white petals, to form a border.

Many of the hardy garden flowers will serve a double purpose in the winter for decoration around the house as they can be dried off indoors and used in flower arrangements. Some flowers need only be picked and hung up in an airy, dry place. Pick the flowers for drying as they open on a day when there has been no dew on the petals. The hydrangea, which is strictly speaking a shrub, has heads that dry very well and among the cottage flowers which will keep all winter through are *Statice limonium*, which is sometimes called sea lavender, with spiky blue flowers very like lavender, and the Chinese lanterns (*Physalis franchetii*) with globe-like seed pods in bright orange. Honesty (*Lunaria annua*) is easy to grow and its silvery pods look attractive at Christmas time after the pretty purple flowers in the summer. The helichrysum family of everlasting flowers has one version that is totally hardy. This is *Helichrysum plicatum* which has silvery-white leaves covered in down and clusters of bright golden-yellow flowers all summer through which dry very well for a sunshine effect in winter. Don't forget old favourites such as the hellebores which will give you flowers in winter and early spring and have dainty picot-edged leaves. For edgings and ground covering, thrift and pinks provide attractive leaves and flowers. Many of the traditional hardy flowers come in a dwarf version — golden rod and michaelmas daisies are two.

Alchemilla mollis

LEAFY PLANTS Foliage plants with attractive marked, coloured or shaped leaves are very important when you are dealing with a small area since they can often be used instead of shrubs or trees to form the skeleton planting, an essential part of the design. Some of them are particularly good in shady corners where few flowers will grow. Hostas are a case in point. They tend to thrive in spots that do not get much light and their handsome leaves are useful for decorating dark corners. Try *Hosta fortunei* or *Hosta undulata* which has wavy leaves marked with cream. In contrast to these broad-leaved plants there are some attractive grasses which can be grown in small borders round a patio or as graceful centrepieces for tubs — *Phalaris arundinacea* 'Picta', otherwise known as gardener's garters has clumps of white striped leaves, or *Hakonechloa*.

But green and white are just part of the colour spectrum when it comes to choosing leafy plants, for there is a whole range of silver and grey to pick from too — the furry lamb's tongue *Stachys lanata*, for instance, senecios and the blue-grey colour of rue, *Ruta graveolens* and *Anthemis cupaniana* with fine grey aromatic leaves. Leaf shapes can range from the very large to the very small. The ornamental rhubarb can make a bold foliage display, for instance; *Rheum palmatum rubram* has red/purple leaves, and the smaller *Rheum alexandrae* has glossy green leaves.

Hosta fortunei

Hakonechloa 'Macro alboaurea'

At the other end of the scale there are ornamental ivies that look good on balconies or in window boxes, some of them variegated in colour like *Hedera* 'Goldheart' which has yellow-gold centres to its leaves or *Hedera canariensis variegata* 'Gloire de Marengo' which has olive green leaves with white edgings that become flecked with crimson. Thistles look handsome as specimen plants and the giant cardoon, *Cynara scolymus*, makes a good substitute for a tree or a shrub in a tub, especially if it is underplanted with silvery-leaved prostrate plants like *Anaphalis nubigena*.

For a really exotic look, you can't beat *Fatsia japonica* with its glossy green leaves that belong more to an indoor than an outdoor plant in this part of Europe. The sword-like leaves of the yucca also give an exotic look, and another candidate for a tub or a terrace is *Arundinaria viridistriata*, the tufted, variegated bamboo which grows between 90-180cm (3-6ft) high. Also consider the red-hot poker family of plants, *Kniphofia caulescens* for instance, which is very like the yucca, with woody trunks and blue-green rosettes of foliage above them and, in the autumn, soft coral-red flowers. Another, even bolder version is *Kniphofia northiae* which does best against a south or west wall and has multiple rosettes of wide-bladed leaves.

For free-standing greenery in a small space, you may like to use bonsai trees which come in many colours (see page 94).

BEDDING PLANTS Small space gardeners tend to rely heavily on bedding plants for excitement and summer colour in their plots. These are half-hardy annuals that are raised under glass, then sold in nurseries and street markets in a half grown or, sometimes, almost flowering stage. There is no reason, however, why you should not raise your own from seed and save money if you have the space to start them off indoors. Starting at soil level, the chorus line so to speak of the bedding plant show, is trailing lobelia and alyssum, both easily found in local nurseries and forming useful underplanting if they are close-packed. Then come the middle ranks. African marigolds (*Tagetes*) are best sellers here, along with busy lizzies (*Impatiens*) which you can now buy in a double white form. Petunias can always be relied upon to give a good colourful show and calceolarias, those purse-shaped spotted flowers, are easily bought too.

In early spring, before these are available, you can brighten up a window box or patio corner with primula, which come in all sorts of bright colours and can always be relied upon to give a good display. The stars of the summer show are geraniums (there are new varieties to raise from seed if you have the space) and fuchsias which will continue to bloom away indefinitely provided you see they have plenty of water. These of course can be overwintered and brought out again next year if you have the storage space for them.

Asters, antirrhinums, stocks and sweet Williams are a good choice of bedding plant if you want a cottage garden look, while on a smaller scale fibrous begonias, *Begonia semperflorens*, give an incredibly good return for your financial outlay since they really do go on flowering all summer through and have unusual, almost bronze leaves. Salvias with their spikes of red flowers make a worthwhile contribution to a raised bed or a window box.

A number of indoor plants too can be considered as candidates for places where you would normally use bedding plants, in boxes or in hanging baskets for instance. It's a good idea to use houseplants of the more robust kind as bedding plants during the summer, provided you remember to bring them indoors in the autumn.

Having purchased your plants, separate them carefully from each other if they are grown together in a tray, breaking as few roots as possible, and set them in place. Make sure that you water them well in until they are established. Remember that in high summer, or in a sunny situation, a hanging basket that has been planted up with bedding specimens will need watering every day, and sometimes night and morning.

It is important to plan a succession of colour for the summer rather than a quick burst of splendour. Avoid plants that need a long time before they flower. Remember shape too. It is best to put the tallest plants at the back of a border graduating down to the trailers at the front.

Mixed border of annuals including pansies and alyssum.
Annuals in amongst permanent patio plants include lobelia and nasturtium.

MINIATURE ROCK GARDENS An old stone sink or a reconstituted stone trough from a garden supplier makes a perfect site, in a small area, to plant a landscape in miniature using alpine plants and tiny conifers for the purpose. Siting the trough is the first important decision to make because once it has been planted, it will be extremely difficult to move around. A large piece of tufa stone — a light, porous limestone — can be used as a sink garden on its own. The surface is quite soft and can be punctured with holes to support young seedlings or rooted cuttings of those alpines which require good drainage. The corner of a balcony or a sunny spot on a patio makes an ideal place, bearing in mind that this kind of planting needs plenty of sun.

To get the best effect, the container needs to be raised about 60cm (2ft) above ground level, so that you are able to view the plants easily. Make sure it has adequate drainage facilities — alpines hate wet soil conditions — and make sure that these drainage holes are not obstructed when you put in a 5-7cm (2-3in) layer of rubble, pebbles or broken crocks. It is a good idea, too, to put a few pieces of barbecue charcoal in to keep the soil sweet. Next there should be a layer of compressed peat or upturned grass turves to give a solid sub-soil. Then finally cover with soil which should ideally be a mix of loam, sand, peat and some grit, into which you set the decorative pieces of rock. If you are using genuine rocks make sure that the strata runs in the same direction to imitate nature as convincingly as possible. If weight is a problem, as it might be on a balcony, then tufa stone, which is light and porous, and can be bought from most garden suppliers, can be substituted for the rock. Ram the soil down thoroughly, leave it to settle for about a week if possible, then you are ready to plant.

Start with the small evergreen trees — the Noah's ark tree, *Juniperus communis* 'Compressa', makes a good focal point. Two other good choices are *Chamaecyparis pisifera* 'Compacta', another miniature conifer, and *Picea abies*

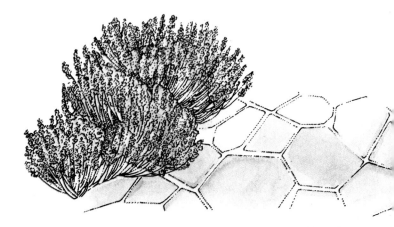

'Nidiformis'. A miniature box from Japan, *Buxus microphylla koreana*, makes another good choice for a trough garden giving it a miniature landscape.

Then you can fill in with flowering plants: Alpine hybrids of dianthus such as Little Jock with pink flowers. Blue Hills has blue-green leaves and carmine flowers. Another good choice is Dr. Hanello with rosy-red blooms. Many familiar names appear in the list of tiny alpines; *Potentilla verna* 'Nana' for instance, which has simple yellow flowers, or *Geranium dalmaticum*, the miniature cranesbill with light pink blooms. Gypsophila comes in an ultra-small form, *Gypsophila repens* 'Dorothy Teacher'. The vivid blue flowers of *Gentiana sino-ornata* are also attractive in this setting and the rosette-like saxifrages and sempervivums make useful fill-ins. Try the colourful *Sempervivum tectorum* 'Triste' or the very attractive 'Jubilee'.

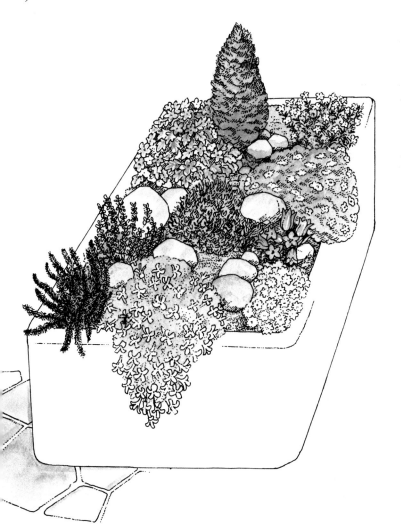

ALPINES AND ROCK GARDEN PLANTS When
space is at a premium, alpines make an ideal way to pack a
large amount of interest into very little room, and provided you
can give them a sunny position, which is what most of them
prefer, they will thrive without too much attention and are able
to cope with an exposed, windy site, a great advantage if you
are gardening on a balcony or a roof patio. A small rock
garden, even if it is housed in a large planter, is an unusual
variation on the conventionally planted box and, raised off the
ground, the specimens are more easily seen and admired.

Since perennial weeds can be a problem with gardens of this
kind (their roots tend to get wedged under pieces of rock), it's
well worth while starting off from the beginning with good
sterilized soil. An ideal mix is two parts loamy soil, one part
coarse sand, one part peat plus John Innes base fertilizer. A
rock garden site should be well drained too, and the easiest
way to achieve this is to have a layer of rubble, clinker or
pebbles at the base.

Alpines are usually at their best in early summer, but if you
choose the right varieties you can have a mix that will flower
from February right through to October. Don't forget that they
will grow well between flagstones on a patio and many of them
will double for useful ground cover too, ajuga for instance.
Ajuga reptans 'Multicolour' has colourful foliage in bronze-
orange and purple and spikes of blue flowers. Some of the
most popular alpines, the gentians, have attractive blue
trumpet-like flowers and saxifrages are also good-natured
plants. Houseleeks (sempervivums) will thrive even in the most
arid places, while *Veronica cataractae*, with its blue flowers,
is not only useful in rock gardens but as a crevice plant on a
patio wall too. A tiny version of the potentilla, *P.
tommasiniana*, will reward you with yellow flowers in early
summer and makes a good carpeter or plant for wall crevices.
Aubrietia, provided it is not allowed to become too straggly, is
a useful and tough rock garden or wall candidate, so is
Campanula 'Birch Hybrid', a version of the harebell that has a
carpeting habit and small blue flowers. Try the prostrate
veronica, *V. prostrata*, and don't forget that pinks (*Dianthus*)
form attractive hummocks of foliage with pretty flowers in
midsummer.

Alpines are particularly useful for softening up the stark lines
of paving stones, and on low retaining walls where they can be
planted in hollows on the top course of bricks or stone or
encouraged to grow in pockets in the mortar. In a very small
space indeed, a window sill for instance, they can look
attractive planted up in pots or in shallow trays. It is important
to remember that the term 'alpine' does not in this sense refer
merely to plants from an alpine environment. It is used loosely
to include plants that are characterized by their preference for
rock garden conditions, and involves a large number of
versatile, attractive flowers and foliage plants.

Pinks and other pin cushion plants are ideal for planting in paved areas.

PLANTS FOR A WATER GARDEN   Plants for a small space water garden fall into several different categories and it is important to know which is which when you are furnishing a pond. There are the proper pond plants, such as water lilies, which are rooted in muddy soil but whose flowers and leaves float on the surface. These come in a variety of sizes, some of which will, amazingly, grow in just a few centimetres of water. For very small pools look out for the word 'pygmaea' attached to the name; that denotes the fact that it can take as little as a 15cm (6in) depth. Two examples of these are *Nymphaea pygmaea* 'Alba', a white water lily, and *N. pygmaea* 'Helvola', which has yellow flowers. Two other shallow-water versions of the water lily are *N. aurora* which has colourful mottled purple leaves and yellow-orange flowers and *N. laydekeri* 'Fulgens' which has crimson blooms. Marginal aquatic plants, like the iris, need to be rooted in mud but in their case the major part of the plant must be out of water, so they are usually planted on a

Nymphaea

shallow shelf round the side of a pond where they serve a useful purpose of disguising plastic linings. The marsh marigold (*Caltha palustris*) is a good choice for a marginal plant and has white as well as yellow flowers. Water forget-me-nots (*Myosotis palustris*) are another attractive marginal plant to choose. The water irises, such as *Iris laevigata* with blue, pink or white flowers, look good decorating the edge of a pond and so do sedge and rush plants which have similar tall spiky leaves.

No pond, however small, should be without some underwater oxygen plants which may not be seen but do a splendid job keeping the water clean and sweet. The water violet (*Hottonia palustris*) shows its violet flowers above the water and so does the water crowfoot (*Ranunculus aquatilis*) which has tiny white flowers. Round the sides of the pond, if the ground is suitable, you could have an attractive display of bog plants which need soil that never dries out. The easiest way to achieve this condition is to line a pocket of soil with polythene and keep it topped up with water when you attend to the pond. Some of the iris family, notably *Iris sibirica*, make good candidates for a waterside garden made in this way. Indeed if you don't have space for a pond you could try a bog garden instead.

WATER GARDENS

Few extras give more pleasure than water in a garden, especially in a small space when it is appreciated all the more. Almost anyone can find the room for a tiny pond, a small fountain to give that extra dimension of constant change and movement and a chance to grow some unusual plants. Indeed some of the smallest water lilies grow in just a few centimetres of water.

If you have room for a pond, as such, the cheapest way to achieve one is to dig a hole and line it with heavy-duty polythene. This can work particularly well on a patio, for instance, where if you have flagstones or marked out squares it is a relatively simple matter to miss one out, dig a hole in the space and line it with polythene before the rest of the paving stones are laid. Free-form ponds made from fibreglass are relatively cheap and easy to find, but in a confined space their wavy shapes may pose problems when you are trying to fit them in. Think in terms of some other container instead — an empty water tank for instance or a deep stone sink. Pools are even possible on balconies: a wooden tub lined with plastic (sometimes you can find a bucket that will fit) can house a water lily. And large urns made from fibreglass, provided their drainage holes are blocked, make rather splendid small space ponds too. Remember that water is heavy and will put a considerable strain on your patio.

If you are making your own pool from plastic sheeting, it pays to step the sides gradually so that you can put in some marginal plants with their roots just in the water. They will also soften the outline a little so that the plastic becomes virtually invisible.

Fountains are very attractive and can be bought with a variety of heads ranging from a single column of water to a spray. Obviously the wider the water is flung, the wider base you need underneath to catch it — a point to bear in mind when buying. An attractive alternative to a fountain is a trickle of water running over a tray of pebbles, or coming from a lion's head or a mask fixed on a wall. Most fountain pumps have an attachment so that they can be used in this way. What is needed is a waterproof basin to catch the water so that it can be siphoned up again. Do be sure in summer to top up the water supply when the fountain pump is used in this way, as it tends to evaporate more quickly than in the case of a conventional pool. You could stock your mini-pond with water lilies but bear in mind that they do not usually thrive in the company of a fountain or running water, they are much happier in still water.

The ideal depth for a small patio pool is 60cm (2ft) deep with a marginal area about 15-20cm (6-8in) deep for shallow water plants. If you are making your own with plastic sheeting, you will find the job is much easier if you line the hole with sand first, so that the plastic has something even and fine-grained to rest on as a base.

Iris pseudacorus as a marginal plant in a water garden.

SUCCESSFUL CROPS IN A SMALL SPACE It's
amazing how many mini crops of fruit and vegetables you can
cram into a very small space with a little careful planning.
Salads in particular, which give a quick return in terms of time
and look decorative, can be kept going all summer in tubs or
window boxes, or better still in raised beds alongside a patio
that still leaves space for some flowers.

The secret lies in the right choice of variety and the practice
of sowing in succession, small amounts of seed weekly or
fortnightly, so that you never have a glut and your space is
maximized. Runner beans, for instance, can be raised in pots
indoors then put into the ground as soon as the danger of frost
is past, taking over space from, say, broad beans which have
finished cropping. Runner beans incidentally are particularly
versatile and can also line patio or balcony walls decoratively
as well as giving you food. Don't forget that you can buy
varieties of runners with pink or white flowers as well as red:
Sunset, for instance, which has pretty pink blooms, and White
Achievement, which not only has white flowers but white
beans as well. They make good temporary screening or they
can be used as the centrepiece in a small space, trained up
bamboos or strings tied wigwam fashion in a formal Versailles
tub (right) or in a small round patio bed.

Colour can be used when growing vegetables in a small
space. Variegated kale has leaves of pink, white and purple. It
is also hardy and will crop into the winter when fresh
vegetables are so scarce. (See pages 82–3.)

Cropping successfully in a small space means a careful
choice of variety. Little Gem, the small individual-sized lettuce,
is easier to tuck away between flowers in a tub for instance, or
you could grow them in individual pots. Salad Bowl is another
good small space variety which does not heart but can be used
on a cut-and-come again basis. Bush tomatoes, particularly the
new popular cherry-sized ones such as Sweet 100 or
Gardener's Delight, are ideal for a small space as they will grow
happily in pots or in hanging baskets where they could be
edged with trailers like peas which will grow anywhere the
sweet pea will survive. Growing bags (see page 20) can be
pressed into temporary service in summer to grow vegetables,
lining the site of a patio or the edge of a balcony to grow
peppers, courgettes, tomatoes and all sorts of half-hardy fruits.
These could be underplanted, as indeed could a floral display
in a tub, with alpine strawberries grown as ground cover.

If you are using the soil in tubs and boxes constantly to
produce intensive crops, it is vital that you fertilize it
frequently. Don't forget to pack in some climbing fruit and
vegetables if you have some space, cucumbers or melons if you
have a sheltered sunny spot. Protect your crops with cloches as
much as possible to bring them on so they are ready before
they become cheap in the shops, that way you get the best
value for money.

Runner beans

DECORATIVE VEGETABLES A large number of vegetables that we now take for granted at the table were once grown purely for decoration — runner beans and rhubarb for instance. So it is not surprising that many of them make a decorative addition to a small space garden and can be grown for their colour or their shape as well as their produce. The globe artichoke is one example of an attractive foliage plant. It is a member of the thistle family and its flower heads make a delicious hors d'oeuvre. Don't attempt to raise artichokes from seed since they will not come true to form. Instead plant suckers taken from a parent plant in the spring, bought from a specialist grower. They like plenty of sun and a rich well-drained soil and in a patio, for instance, they make interesting specimen plants in tubs since they need planting 60cm (24in) apart.

Asparagus, with its attractive feathery foliage, makes a good background plant in a large raised bed if you can spare the space for a trench. Many herbs and vegetables make attractive edgings in a small plot, parsley, for instance, which can be bought in loose and curly leafed forms, in a Japanese version and a wild version too. Chives will multiply quickly and can stand a certain amount of shade. Don't let them flower if you want to use them for cooking, they lose much of their onion flavour. Courgettes, allowed to scramble over a piece of mesh

Globe artichoke

Courgette in flower

or trained up bamboo sticks, also look attractive, especially if you mix them in with nasturtiums whose flower colours echo theirs.

Two other attractive foliage plants well worth putting into the garden are rhubarb which makes a striking specimen if it is underplanted with bedding flowers, and Swiss chard which is a member of the beetroot family and has lovely silver and dark green leaves. The curly leaved endive (*Cichorium endivia*) is a useful plant since its leaves can be eaten in autumn when lettuce may be dying down. Chinese cabbage and other oriental greens also make a contribution to a small garden. Look out for the edible chrysanthemum for instance. Peppers and aubergines can be grown very successfully in the shelter of a patio or a window box though they need to be started off indoors since they are not hardy. Their fruits will ripen happily most years and look decorative grown up a trellis or with the plant tied to a stake.

Since most vegetables are grown as annuals, there is a good opportunity to switch round from year to year, trying different items for decorative effect; radishes, for example, make a useful, quick-growing border in a spot where you intend to put some bedding plants later on.

There is a good opportunity to involve children in the cultivation of vegetables on the patio. They can plant seeds or cuttings in window boxes and watch foliage or even crops grow from them. Beans, avocado stones, garlic bulbs and herb cuttings are ideal.

84 ATTRACTIVE AND USEFUL HERBS

There are all sorts of spaces in a small garden plot, even if it is little more than a window sill, where you have the chance to grow useful and attractive herbs for the kitchen. Containers can be pressed into service ranging from a terra cotta parsley or strawberry pot to a tub, and some herbs, bay for instance, make a decorative contribution to the scene on their own.

If space is at a premium, then stick to parsley and the six basic herbs: marjoram, mint, thyme, tarragon, sage and chives, sowing annuals such as borage or dill to fill in the odd spots. Basil is another important herb to have and is treated in this part of Europe as a half-hardy annual. A pot purchased in late spring can sit on a sunny window sill right through to the first frosts in October, giving you a constant crop of its aromatic leaves.

Of the six basic herbs, mint is the best known, and the most difficult to control since it will rampage over any plot in which it is planted. For this reason it is best coralled in some way: the traditional method in an open bed is to grow it in a bottomless bucket sunk into the ground. In a small space, the best solution is to keep it on its own in a large pot, alternating with a few

Container-grown bay tree

spring bulbs for seasonal colour. The rest of the six will live happily together in a mixed planter. The larger lesser known herbs like lemon balm (*Melissa officinalis*), lovage (*Ligusticum scoticum*) and angelica (*Angelica archangelica*) tend to loom large in a raised bed but make splendid specimen plants put on their own in tubs with ground cover around them.

Most herbs prefer a sunny spot but there are a few that will thrive in the shade — comfrey (*Symphytum officinale*), for example. Mint (*Mentha*) will also survive in a shady spot but sun-lovers such as tarragon would be unhappy in similar circumstances. Thymes (*Thymus*) are good value and come in several attractive prostrate varieties.

Many herbs have attractive coloured foliage and you could have an all-gold bed with golden lemon thyme (*Thymus citriodorus* 'Aureus'), golden marjoram (*Origanum vulgare* 'Aureum'), golden feverfew (*Chrysanthemum parthenium* 'Golden Ball') and ginger mint, which is variegated with yellow. In fact with a little thought you can have a really colourful herb patch by picking special variations of your favourite plants. Purple basil makes a marvellous showpiece and sage (*Salvia*) comes in a purple and a tricolour version. When the autumn comes and the first frosts arrive, it is a good idea to dig up pieces of root of your favourite perennial herbs and bring them indoors. Planted in a pot in a warm room they will spring to life again.

Assorted thymes in a tub

SMALL SCALE HERB GARDENS Herbs normally look at their best when they are grown in a formal setting, so they lend themselves particularly well to being grown in window boxes or containers or used on a patio. In the middle ages, they were often laid out in formal knot gardens or parterres and an attractive modification of this can be achieved on a balcony by having four triangular beds, each with a different set of herbs in them, placed in the four corners. The same idea could be used on a patio. You could even create a moveable mini-knot garden by arranging a series of matching window boxes on the ground so that they form a pattern. On a much simpler scale, a variety of herbs all grown in pots of different sizes can be grouped together in the corner of a patio or on a disused flower bed to make an attractive picture. In Mediterranean countries you will see large stone pots of herbs or even disused metal cans painted to match each other, lining an outdoor stairway to a balcony, catching the best of the sun.

One of the simplest but most effective herb gardens on a patio is in the shape of a chequerboard, alternating flagstones with squares of thickly growing herbs. This works particularly well with the more prostrate varieties like low-growing versions of thyme and mint or pennyroyal, for instance. A window box planted with herbs looks attractive and is a practical proposition as well, since you can simply lean out of the kitchen window and cut what you want. If space is really a

problem then consider investing in tower pots, containers that lock into one another, skyscraper fashion. Each can be planted with different types of herbs but do bear in mind that it is essential to make sure your tower is level, otherwise when you water it from the top, some pockets of plants may miss out.

Herbs require a moderately rich soil since many of them are perennial plants and will not be moved from their planted position. If they are being planted in containers or in raised beds you should incorporate plenty of organic matter.

For their general health and for ease of maintenance, herbs are best grown together and you can use prostrate versions of thyme, for instance, as trailers to soften the edges of a tub. One of the most attractive ways to grow herbs on a small scale is in a white painted tub which shows off their attractive foliage to perfection. Raised beds of herbs also look very good, and if you have a circular bed in which to grow them, an old cartwheel partially sunk into the soil makes an ideal way to divide one kind of plant from another. Another place where they can be grown is in pockets of soil on top of a low brick wall.

Most herbs are easy to propagate from cuttings and you can soon build up a collection of small bushy plants to use as edgings. Chives (*Allium schoenoprasum*), winter savory (*Satureia montana*), cotton lavender (*Santolina chamaecyparissus*), marjoram (*Origanum vulgare*) are all good candidates for this treatment.

TRAINED FRUIT AND VINES
Fruit for the patio is best produced on strictly trained trees and bushes. They take up little room, always look neat, and produce more fruit than the uncontrolled growth of the usual garden trees.

Most fruit trees can be trained up or alongside walls and fences to take advantage of the extra shelter and warmth they give, and to cut down the room they take up. Blackcurrants are the one exception. Because they produce on young wood, they must be grown as a 'stool', rather like a bush rose. The rest can all be grown flat against a wall. The fig is the ideal fruit for the patio, since its roots have to be restricted if it is to produce figs instead of a lot of vegetation. It can be fan trained by tying in to horizontal wires on the wall. Plums can also be grown fan trained on a wall or fence. Tie each shoot onto a cane and spread them out in a fan shape, tying the canes to wires on the wall. After four years the canes can be removed. Cherries can be trained in the same way. Sweet cherries are difficult, because they grow very big, they take a long time to come into bearing and they need cross-pollination with another cherry. But the sour Morello cherry is self-fertile, comes into bearing early, and does not grow so big. It also has the advantage of preferring a north wall, so as to delay flowering until after any frosts.

Apples and pears can be grown as small bushes, but as they get bigger they take up a lot of room for the amount of fruit

Grapes on a patio vine

produced. Much better to grow these fruits as neat, compact cordons. These are single-stemmed trees which bear early and produce a lot of fruit in very little space. They can be grown upright, but if they are trained at a diagonal they fruit better, and also take up less height. You can get double and triple cordons, shaped like candelabra, and espaliers, which have a short, upright trunk with horizontal branches coming off both sides. Gooseberries and redcurrants are also happy as diagonal cordons. Nurseries charge more for these trained trees, and you can cut the cost by getting one-year-old trees and training them yourself, but it is not as easy as it looks, and what you are paying for is the nurseryman's skill and time in training the tree.

   Vines are happy on patios, as they like the sheltered environment, but they must have their roots in the soil — they will never do well in a container since they normally send their roots down 6m (20ft). Buy a one-year-old plant, and allow the top two buds to grow on as shoots, rubbing out the rest. Do this every year until it gets to where you want it to fruit. For a patio vineyard you will probably not crop enough grapes for wine making so dual purpose cultivars should be chosen which provide grapes for wine making and cooking and eating. Suitable cultivars include Precose de Malingre, an early white grape; the standard blue Concorde; Muscat de Saumur, a golden muscat flavoured grape; and Gagarin Blue.

CARE OF FRUIT TREES AND VINES

Grape vines fruit on the previous year's growth and have to be pruned every winter. Remove the shoots that have just finished fruiting and tie in the previous summer's new shoots, which will fruit in the coming season. Routine disease control is to dust with sulphur against powdery mildew, and spray with zineb against downy mildew.

Trained apples should be pruned in winter and summer. In August, side growths are shortened to five leaves, and in the winter, they are cut to two buds and leading growths are shortened by a third. Fruit should be thinned in July. Give a winter wash against pests, and spray captan fortnightly from April to August.

Pears are treated similarly, but they can be pruned rather harder. Plums should not be grown as cordons, but can be fan trained, and do well against a west wall. Each winter shorten the main branches to produce more ribs to the fan until the whole wall is covered. After that, keep your pruning to a minimum just to reduce disease risk. A winter DNOC wash is the only pest control needed. Peaches and nectarines are best fan trained like plums but they should be given a south wall if possible, if not, a west wall. Thin peaches in July to one fruit per 23cm (9in) of wood to produce good-sized fruit. Spray in

A fan trained *Prunus cerasus* 'Morello'.

February with Bordeaux mixture against peach leaf curl.

Morello cherries can be fan trained on a north wall, in a similar way to plums. But they fruit only on the previous year's wood, so once the fan framework is established, some of the old wood — two, three or four years old — must be cut out each year to encourage new young fruiting growth. They should be given a routine tar oil wash each winter. Figs can be trained to a rough fan shape on a south wall, or as a bush in a sheltered corner of two walls. They fruit on the previous summer's shoots, and to encourage this, new growth should be stopped at the fifth leaf. Do not feed unless a heavy crop is carried, but give plenty of water. Figs are not completely hardy, and in a severe winter they should be covered with straw or something similar. They are normally disease-free.

Gooseberries and red and white currants can be grown as single, double or triple cordons. In winter, shorten leaders by a third and cut side shoots to two buds. In summer, prune laterals back to five leaves. Routine pest control is not usually needed. To get good-sized dessert gooseberries, thin the fruit in June to one every 2cm (1in) of wood. Strawberries are easy to grow, but need a lot of feeding. Alpine strawberries without runners are the tidiest, but you may have to net them against birds, even on a patio or balcony.

SOFT FRUIT IN CONTAINERS To most people the idea of growing soft fruit in pots or containers is confined to strawberries which undoubtedly look decorative in purpose-made clay pots or in barrels. If you are making your own strawberry barrel, do remember that drainage is vital — bore holes in the bottom of the barrel as well as the sides, stand it on some bricks to allow the water to run free, make sure that it is on a level surface so that all the plants get their share of moisture and, above all, put in a central core of gravel or pebbles to assist drainage and to help stop the compost from going sour. As you fill the barrel, place a piece of plastic drainpipe in the centre and fill with pebbles too, pulling the pipe up, gradually, as you go. Discontinue this drainage system about 15cm (6in) below the top of the barrel, fill in with more compost and plant runners on the top. Water as the plants are growing. Strawberries are susceptible to virus diseases so choose disease-free specimens and renew plants after two or three crops. To propagate, select runners which are produced by most varieties from June onwards and plant them in some John Innes No. 1 ready for the next season. Strawberries can also be grown in hanging baskets.

The strawberry cultivar choice is wide. Of the standard cultivars, Redgauntlet, Cambridge Favourite, Royal Sovereign, or Templar can be grown, but the everbearing cultivars seem more suited for container work. Frapendula, Gento, Remont, Ozark Beauty, Streamliner and Ogallala are suitable ever-bearers fruiting from mid-June to a peak in the autumn.

Figs make attractive container plants and can be grown very successfully this way as their roots need to be restricted before they will fruit. Brown Turkey is the most usual choice of fig, and it can be kept happily out of doors in a sheltered sunny spot, preferably against a wall. However, if there is a chance of snow or a really hard frost, the shoots must be protected. It is safer to bring the fig in, so a barrel on castors is a good solution for this particular fruit.

The blackberry makes a useful wall cover plant, the usual spined variety serving as an excellent 'hitching post' for climbers such as clematis to hook themselves to. However, if it is to be grown in a place where people could brush against it, then choose 'Oregon Thornless' which has attractive, deeply indented leaves and, of course, no thorns to catch on clothing. Plant blackberry canes any time from late autumn through to early spring, cutting them back to about 25cm (10in) to give them a vigorous start in life, and at the end of the season, cut off any canes that have fruited right down to the base for they fruit on fresh growth produced during the previous year. The same method of pruning goes for raspberries which are another soft fruit that make surprisingly good container candidates. During their period of summer growth they can be ringed with garden twine to stop them sprawling, thus leaving space for bedding and trailing plants to circle the soil below.

When you are pruning, leave no more than six or seven new shoots to fruit. This is done in the spring when you can survey the plants and decide which canes to keep and which must go. There are several other versions of the raspberry/blackberry family available now, including a new plant called the tayberry. When you are dealing with limited space it is more fun often to try something unusual like this. Another soft fruit idea is to grow alpine strawberries in pots and bring them to the table for guests to pick their own.

Strawberries in a wooden barrel

94 BONSAI TREES

Many people think that bonsai trees and shrubs are items to be grown indoors, but nothing could be further from the truth. Although specimens can be brought into the house from time to time for a few days, they would quickly die if they were not kept permanently outside since they are nothing more than miniaturized and prematurely aged versions of woodland trees. This makes them ideal candidates for patios, and balconies in particular where space is at a premium, and they can do well too on an outdoor window sill. Traditionally bonsai are displayed on staging or shelves since they need to be seen at eye level to be appreciated properly. If you have the patience to do so, growing these dwarfed trees can become a fascinating hobby, but it is now possible to buy ready-grown specimens from bonsai specialists who import them from Japan. If you intend to try your hand at bonsai, you should read one of the specialist books on the subject.

Remember that a bonsai tree is simply a miniature version of an ordinary outdoor tree and needs the same basic treatment. It needs nourishment and water — never let the container dry out. A decorative wall display of bonsai would look particularly good on the side wall of a balcony or a patio, against a white background. Choose simple but colourful containers for your specimens. Choose pots of a capacity that is two-thirds of the tree's height. Bonsai trees in their early stages usually stay in the same container for two years, so bear this in mind when choosing them.

A bonsai chamaecyparis

INDEX

Numbers in italics refer to illustrations